Published by Fortyfive Design Ltd
Wellington, New Zealand

This publication is designed and
printed in Wellington, New Zealand

ISBN 978-0-473-41921-9

Design © Fortyfive Design Ltd 2018
Photography © Fortyfive Design Ltd 2018
Text © Fortyfive Design Ltd 2018

CONCEPT | DESIGN
TEXT | PHOTOGRAPHY
Liane McGee, Anna Vibrandt
Niki Chu and Andrew McGee

PRINTER
Blue Star Print Group

PAPER
Printed on Sapphire Offset,
a PEFC certified stock supplied
by Spicers New Zealand

www.fortyfive.co.nz
Email: info@fortyfive.co.nz
Instagram: @cuba_street_cookbook

CUBA STREET

A COOKBOOK

Liane McGee, Niki Chu and Anna Vibrandt

CONTENTS

ENJOY A TASTE OF CUBA

Take a journey with us up Cuba Street as we serve a selection of stories and tastes from some of its best-loved places. *Cuba Street – a cookbook* **is about Wellington hospitality and the food we love to eat. It's also about a district with a strong sense of community, famous for its diversity and flavour.**

In this book you'll find some of the best Cuba Street has to offer – from street food to street parties! We'll also take some detours along the way, to meet up with friends and family.

Cuba Street has had many evolutions over the years. It was one of the earliest streets to be established in Te Aro, surveyed in the 1840s and named after the settler ship *Cuba*, which had arrived in Wellington in 1840. The district has always been the working end of Wellington, bustling with businesses that have fed, clothed and entertained people well before the European settlers named it.

Originally running from Vivian Street to Manners Street, in the 1850s Cuba Street was extended southwards to where it ends today, at Webb Street. Cuba Street's late-Victorian and early-Edwardian architecture reflects the building boom that helped establish its character.

In 1969, with the creation of Cubacade – one of the first malls in New Zealand – part of the street became pedestrian-only and the iconic bucket fountain was installed. Today Cuba Street occupies seven blocks and is home to around 40 heritage buildings.

Although it was named after a ship, Cuba Street is identified most of all with the country of the same name, channelling the shabby grandeur and bright colours of Havana, and celebrating the heroes of the Cuban revolution in the names of its cafés and eateries. Some would say that Cuba Street has created a revolution of its own – bringing to the people of Wellington great food and atmosphere: a heady mix of fine and informal dining, cool music and great vibes. Viva Cuba! – we love you!

Left: Niki Chu, Liane McGee and Anna Vibrandt

Fortyfive Design Studio is a graphic design company based in Wellington
www.fortyfive.co.nz

WELLINGTON NIGHT MARKETS

Inspired by the night markets of her home country, Lily Kao set up the Wellington Night Markets as a weekly celebration of street food, culture and creativity. The markets bring to Cuba Street a diverse range of international cuisine and family-friendly entertainment.

Lily Kao's story is surprising. Originally from Taiwan, Lily studied German at Auckland University and after graduating with a Master's degree, moved to Wellington to look for work. Instead, she found love. Settling down to married life with a baby, Lily no longer wanted to follow a typical career path, instead deciding to create something she could enjoy with her daughter Yuli and which would bring with it a little of her culture from home. In Taiwan night markets are everywhere, offering quality street food and rich cultural experiences, things Lily felt Wellington lacked when she first explored the idea of setting up a market here.

Lily's family has been in the restaurant business for over 60 years, and while Lily vowed never to go into hospitality, it was a huge part of her upbringing. Growing up, she was always encouraged to try new foods, and her ongoing curiosity is central to her love of the markets. Initially she saw the night markets as predominantly Asian, but soon realised they should celebrate a diversity of cultures and cuisines.

She actively seeks out and supports new food ideas from potential stall owners. The night markets encourage people new to the food business to give it a try, and Lily provides advice and marketing support for fledgling businesses. Many small food stalls that start here go on to grow into successful businesses.

When Lily first decided to set up the night markets, people were discouraging. But Lily's husband, who'd lived in Wellington for over 18 years, was positive and encouraged her with the notion that "it's Cuba Street, it will work". Admittedly, the city has its challenges. The weather doesn't always work in the markets' favour, especially the Saturday market at the bottom of Cuba Street. This location can be a wind tunnel on a particularly blustery day, and the market set-up team always keeps a close eye on the forecast building up to the weekend. Although the markets really come into their own in the warmer months, they're still well supported even when the weather is not so good. There's a definite camaraderie among the die-hard market-goers in winter!

Right: Lily Kao

The night markets started with the Friday market in the Left Bank Arcade, part-way up Cuba Street. Every Friday from 5pm it fills up with thousands of hungry locals and visitors. Its success meant it needed to expand, but that part of Cuba Street had little space for more. That's how the Saturday market came about, in 2014. The bottom of Cuba Street could be blocked off from traffic and provided a generous open space. Having a market there was also a way to get more foot traffic down the quieter end of the street.

The night markets provide scope for a wide range of stall owners, but the focus is mainly on street food. From students selling deep-fried ice cream, to established food trucks, the Friday market has about 20 stalls and the Saturday market 30 or more. During special events such as CubaDupa, the number of stalls can increase to over 40. It's estimated that around 750,000 people visit the markets each year.

Entertainment is a huge part of the night market ethos. Most events aim to encourage families to join in. In the past there's been a bubble day, a snow weekend (with a snow machine), and there are plans to hold a massive pillow-fight to coincide with International Pillow-Fight Day on 1 April. There are over 200 live music performances every year. The market also offers opportunities for fundraising, and supports local talent and community groups.

Last year the Wellington Night Markets and Lily's daughter Yuli both celebrated their fifth birthday. Yuli loves the fact that the markets are as old as she is!

Right: Yuli Martin

MR CIRCLE

Having worked as an architectural and 3D designer for over eight years, Dong Zhang (the man behind Mr Circle) was looking for a new challenge, one that would take him out of the office and away from the computer. He was attracted to the visual appeal of the popular Chinese street food jianbing, a type of crêpe often eaten for breakfast by students and office workers.

Jianbing are one of the oldest Chinese street foods, thought to have originated around 220–280 AD in the Shandong Province when soldiers used their shields to cook a basic batter of wheat and water, as their woks had been destroyed in battle.

When deciding what to call his new business, Dong first hit upon Try It, then played around with the name of the crêpe and came up with Mr Jianbing. But when a design colleague suggested Mr Circle, referring to the shape of the crêpes and the hot plate they're cooked on, the name stuck. On his first day of business, Dong was unprepared for the huge response. The crêpes are made on a rotating hot plate and require a lot of practice to get right – the early days saw a lot of egg flying! He's now perfected the art of making this deliciously spicy and crunchy Chinese snack. The fillings have evolved largely from customer feedback and suggestions, with the most popular filling, pork belly, simply being a case of using up leftovers. Regardless of the fillings, the important thing has been to keep the flavours authentically Chinese. Jianbing are proving so popular that Mr Circle is now at the Capital Market and the Harbourside Market.

Dong has found that with taking the plunge and setting up a business he's discovered a new side to himself – a much more sociable side. He loves the energy and atmosphere of the night markets, and has made more friends in three months than he would have in three years working at a desk.

Left: Dong Zhang   Right: Tina Xia

MR CIRCLE'S CHINESE CRÊPE

CHICKEN JIANBING

STIR-FRIED CHICKEN BREAST | In a large bowl combine the garlic, soy sauce, water, honey, 1 tablespoon of the oil, cornflour, black pepper and chilli flakes. Cut the chicken into strips and place in the marinade. Cover and refrigerate for 2 hours, stirring the chicken after an hour.

In a large skillet, heat the remaining tablespoon of oil. Transfer the chicken to the hot skillet using a slotted spoon, reserving the marinade. Stir-fry the chicken for 5 minutes, then add the reserved marinade. Stir for a further 30 seconds or until the sauce thickens. Set aside.

CRÊPES | In a medium bowl, sift and combine all three flours. Once mixed, whisk in the water gradually to form a smooth and creamy batter.

In a small bowl, whisk an egg and put aside. Deep fry the wonton wrappers in oil. Drain and leave to cool.

In a crêpe-pan or large non-stick skillet, warm a teaspoon of the vegetable oil over a medium heat. Pour in about half a cup of the batter and quickly spread around the entire surface of the pan with a bench scraper or large spoon. Cook the crêpe for 1–2 minutes. Once the edges begin to curl, pour the whisked egg onto the crêpe and spread it evenly.

Sprinkle the spring onions, coriander and 1 teaspoon of sesame seeds over the egg. Cook for another minute, until the egg begins to set.

Carefully flip the crêpe over, then brush with 1 tablespoon of hoisin sauce and 1 teaspoon of chilli sauce. Arrange the deep-fried wonton wrappers (broken into small pieces) or potato chips, lettuce and stir-fried chicken down the centre of the wrap. Drizzle with mayonnaise. Fold one side of the crêpe to cover the filling, then gently roll the crêpe over to create a wrap. Cut in half to serve.

Makes 3–5 crêpes

INGREDIENTS

Stir-fried chicken breast

2 large garlic cloves, minced

¼ cup soy sauce

¼ cup water

¼ cup honey

2 tbsp vegetable oil

1 tbsp cornflour

¼ tsp ground black pepper

¼ tsp chilli flakes, or to taste

500g boneless, skinless chicken breast

Crêpe batter

⅓ cup of each: wheat flour, cornflour and yellow pea flour

250ml water

3–5 tsp vegetable oil (for cooking)

Crêpe filling

Wonton wrappers, deep fried (or potato chips)

3–5 eggs

1 lettuce, shredded

1–2 spring onions, finely sliced

1–2 bunches coriander, finely chopped

3–5 tsp black sesame seeds

3–5 tbsp hoisin sauce

3–5 tsp Asian chilli sauce

Mayonnaise

HOUSE OF DUMPLINGS

Vicky Ha is the powerhouse behind the fabulous House of Dumplings, bringing a fresh approach to this classic Asian food. Her authentic dumplings have become a firm favourite at the Wellington Night Markets.

After trying a series of different jobs, Vicky, originally from Hong Kong, hit upon the idea of re-creating the dumplings of her childhood as taught to her by her mother. Encouraged by friends who'd tasted them, Vicky set up a stall at the then Wellington City Market. It took 17 hours to prepare for the first day at the market, and the dumplings sold out in only two. It's been all go since. Two years later, Vicky opened the House of Dumplings on Taranaki Street, a small but perfectly formed café filled to the brim with Hong Kong street style, yummy dumplings, homemade sauces and fresh salads. Although she no longer runs the café, it has become the hub for her thriving business. There, Vicky concentrates on keeping up with the demand for frozen dumplings and sauces, sold at supermarkets nationwide, and prepares the fresh dumplings which she pan-fries at markets and festivals up and down the country.

Vicky's passion for local produce and natural flavours speaks to the heart of homemade rather than commercial cooking. It was very apparent when we went to photograph the food for this book. Surrounded by mountains of beautiful fresh New Zealand produce, it was hard not to get caught up in Vicky's energy and enthusiasm. After three hours of cooking and photographing a new recipe of fish dumplings with karengo seaweed accompanied by greens, our joint enthusiasm for what had just been created spoke volumes. The proof was in the eating!

Left: Vicky Ha

WAREHOU DUMPLINGS WITH KARENGO PASTRY

WAKAME AND KARENGO PASTRY | Place the flour and wakame and karengo seaweed into a bowl or onto a stainless-steel bench, make a well in the middle and pour in the hot water. Stir with a fork until the mixture is hard to move. Knead the dough for about 10 minutes, until smooth. Form into a ball, wrap in cling film, and set aside at room temperature for at least half an hour.

FISH FILLING | While waiting for the pastry to set, mix together all the fish filling ingredients and set aside in the fridge.

DUMPLINGS SKINS | Cut the dough into four parts. Flatten each portion with your palm and dust both sides with flour. To roll out the skins you can either use a pastry machine or rolling pin. The pastry should be 2–3mm thick.

Use a 10cm pastry cutter to cut out the rounds. This recipe makes 30–34 rounds (the leftover pastry can be put through the fettuccine or spaghetti setting of a pasta machine and used in noodle soup).

ASSEMBLING THE DUMPLINGS | Place a tablespoon of filling in the middle of the dumpling skin. Brush a bit of water onto the edge of the skin, fold the skin in half, and pinch the edges with your thumb and fingers to tightly seal the dumpling. Finish by bringing the two corners towards each other and squeezing to join.

The recipe continues on the next page.

Makes 20 dumplings
Dairy free

INGREDIENTS

Wakame and karengo pastry

2 tbsp each of karengo and wakame (we recommend Pacific Harvest)

¾ cup boiling water

2 cups plain flour, sifted

Fish filling

250g blue warehou or any firm white fish, diced 1cm

1 stalk lemongrass, white parts only, finely chopped

1 large shallot, finely diced

¼ knob galangal root, finely chopped

2 small knobs turmeric, finely chopped

5 garlic cloves, finely chopped

1 handful of Vietnamese mint, finely chopped

1 handful of Thai basil, finely chopped

3 kaffir limes leaves, finely chopped

1 kaffir lime, zest

1 tsp ground white pepper

1 tbsp fish sauce

1 tbsp cold-pressed vegetable oil (we use the Good Oil's rapeseed oil)

1 chilli, finely chopped (optional)

COOKING THE DUMPLINGS | Steaming method: Spray the stream trays with oil and steam the dumplings for 5 minutes over boiling water. If you don't have a Chinese bamboo basket for steaming, you can use a metal colander.

Boiling method: Place the dumplings one at a time into boiling water, scooping them out once they start to float.

Pan-frying method: Steam the dumplings first, then pan-fry in a medium-hot oiled pan until both sides of the pastry are caramelised. It should take less than 1 minute for each side.

Serve the dumplings with Shallot and Garlic Dipping Sauce (see recipe below) and a mixture of steamed and grilled seasonal greens.

SHALLOT AND GARLIC DIPPING SAUCE

Heat the oil until medium-hot, then fry the shallot and garlic until golden. Remove from the heat. Add the fish sauce, stir and serve.

This recipe makes enough for a small bowl of dipping sauce.

Dairy free

INGREDIENTS

2 tbsp cold-pressed vegetable oil

1 shallot, finely sliced

2 garlic cloves, finely sliced

1 tbsp fish sauce

106 CUBA STREET
MATTERHORN

Originally established as a tearoom in 1963 by Swiss immigrants Mary and Tony Tresch, the Matterhorn has long played an important part in the Wellington hospitality scene. While some still remember it as the tearoom they were taken to as children, many of us know it as one of Wellington's first and hippest lounge bars.

The Matterhorn has changed hands a number of times since it first opened, but it's probably best known for the incarnation set up in 1997 by Leon Surynt, Sam Chapman, Christian McCabe and Adán Tijerina. Bringing something new to Wellington, it was a place where exotic drinks flowed and staff were unbelievably cool, and it was often ranked among the World's 50 Best Bars. It brought a new style of dining to the city, one that evolved from noodle boxes to award-winning, world-class dining. While the Matterhorn remains true to the lounge bar and restaurant it was in the late 1990s, current owner Sean Marshall has at times found the legend a big legacy to honour.

The Matterhorn goes beyond being a great venue for live music. It has always played a large part in encouraging and inspiring local musicians. Bands and musicians such as L. A. Mitchell, Ladie6 and Fat Freddy's Drop have been influenced by their experiences here, either as performers or punters.

At the time of writing this book, the Matterhorn was looking to close at its current location while the building undergoes earthquake strengthening. The outpouring of support for the Matterhorn shows that Wellington will miss this Cuba Street landmark. Fingers crossed we see another incarnation soon!

Left: Tekapua Hui, Edna Zhou   Right: Imon Starr

LISA TOMLINS

Singer, songwriter and camping enthusiast Lisa Tomlins is well known for her beautiful, soulful voice. She has played in many bands and at many venues, but feels that the Matterhorn has been most influential to her professional life.

Lisa's favourite nights at the Matterhorn were the Soul Emergency sessions with DJs Fonky Monk Matt and Toby Nairobi, who played funky soul on 7-inch vinyl. They were nights of drinking Manhattans and dancing until the wee hours – it was impossible to keep off the dance floor.

For Lisa, the Matterhorn felt something like a haven. It always had a feeling of exclusivity. You'd walk down the long, mysterious passageway, then you'd arrive and instantly be made to feel welcome. It is and was a place made special by its staff.

The Matterhorn provided Lisa with her longest-running residency – over 10 years – with the group The Eggs. They recently reunited to play one last time before the Matterhorn closed its doors. The Eggs are a Wellington super-group featuring members of Fat Freddy's Drop, The Phoenix Foundation and Twinset, who come together to perform their own brand of rhythm and soul.

Having performed and enjoyed great music at the Matterhorn for many years, for Lisa it will always be a special place.

Left: Sam Lindsay, Lisa Tomlins and Chris Yeabsley
Right: Imon Starr, Lucien Johnson and Daniel Yeabsley

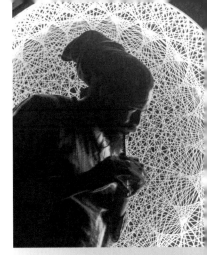

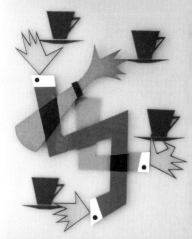

BUTTERMILK CHICKEN

This recipe needs to be prepared a few days in advance.

Day 1: Make the brine and let it cool in the fridge until the next day.
Day 2: Cut the chicken thighs and marinate in the brine (up to 4 hours).
Day 3: Dredge and fry the chicken.

DAY 1: BRINE | In a large pot, mix the salt and water until the salt is dissolved. Add the remaining ingredients and bring to the boil. Simmer 15–20 minutes, until the brine is fragrant. Take the pot off the heat and let it sit at room temperature for a few hours until cool. Strain the brine through a fine sieve and cool further in the fridge until the next day. At Matterhorn we make this in large batches and keep for later use.

DAY 2: CHICKEN | Clean the chicken thighs by trimming off any excess skin, sinew and cartilage. Cut each thigh into 2–3 pieces (you usually get 2 large pieces and 1 smaller piece). Separate the large and small pieces into two bowls – the smaller pieces will brine/cook faster than the larger pieces. Pour brine over the thigh pieces. Brine the small pieces for 2½ hours and the large pieces for 4 hours. While the chicken is in the brine, make the buttermilk marinade.

DAY 2: BUTTERMILK MARINADE | Sift the tapioca flour into a bowl, and add the paprika. Add the remaining ingredients and combine. Cover and let rest in the fridge for 1–2 hours. Strain the chicken pieces and discard the brine. In two large bowls, mix together the chicken pieces and marinade. Cover and let sit in the fridge overnight. You can vacuum pack the chicken to speed up the marinating process.

The recipe continues on the next page.

Serves 8–12

INGREDIENTS

Brine

10 litres cold water

500g salt

10g black peppercorns, whole

2 lemons, cut into slices

3 garlic cloves, lightly crushed

4 bay leaves

1 small bunch of thyme

Chicken

2kg boneless, skinless chicken thighs

Buttermilk marinade

800ml cultured buttermilk

1 tbsp smoked paprika powder

2 tsp tapioca flour

1 bunch coriander, finely chopped

2 garlic cloves, finely grated

2 lemons, zest and juice

1 tsp sea salt flakes

1 tsp cracked pepper

DAY 3: CHICKEN DREDGING FLOUR | In a large bowl, whisk together the flour, seasoning and other dry ingredients. Remove excess marinade from the chicken pieces in a colander. In a large bowl or tray, dredge the chicken pieces in the flour mix, making sure the entire surface of each piece is evenly coated. Let the chicken sit in the flour for about 10 minutes. The marinade and the first coat of flour will form a kind of batter. Dredge the chicken pieces in the flour again, to give them a second coating. Lightly shake off the excess flour and let rest on a wire rack with a tray underneath (this is so you don't make a mess!).

DAY 3: COOKING THE CHICKEN | Heat a pot (or deep-fryer) of canola oil to 165°C. Fry the chicken in small batches so you don't crowd the pot; the pieces shouldn't be touching. Cook the small pieces for 3–4 minutes and the large pieces for 5–6 minutes. An easy way to test if the chicken is done is to use an instant-read thermometer. Once the chicken is at 75°C, shake off the excess oil and place on a wire rack to rest for 3–5 minutes. Serve immediately.

TIP | The trick to get really crispy and flavourful fried chicken is to get the dredging right, especially on the first coating. Take a handful of dredging flour and place a piece of chicken on it. Take another handful of flour and massage it into the chicken, applying pressure to make the flour stick. Most of it will come off, but it'll get a good first coating.

INGREDIENTS

Chicken dredging flour

1kg plain flour

40g smoked paprika powder

35g onion powder

35g garlic powder

10g lemon powder

30g salt

1 tsp cayenne pepper

1 tsp baking powder

1 tsp baking soda

RHUBARB AND SAFFRON NEGRONI

In a chilled glass, add the saffron-infused gin, rhubarb liqueur and Campari. Stir with ice until sufficiently chilled and diluted. Trim the pith from a broad strip of orange peel and express the oils over the drink by gently pinching and rolling. Garnish with a strip of orange peel, or with an orange wedge for a bit more acidity.

SAFFRON-INFUSED GIN | Add 6–8 threads of saffron, depending on the quality and freshness, to a bottle of gin. We recommend a traditional London Dry-style gin (which for us is Tanqueray; but Beefeater, Sipsmith or Bombay would also work). Seal the bottle and rest for 4–5 days at room temperature before using.

RHUBARB LIQUEUR | This part's a bit less scientific – essentially we're making a rhubarb-infused syrup, then cutting it with vodka.

Trim the ends and any root remnants of the rhubarb stalks, and shave lengthwise using a peeler, zester or mandolin. Combine the shaved rhubarb with an equal weight of sugar syrup (which is 2 parts sugar, 1 part water by weight), and vacuum pack. A zip-lock bag or other airtight storage will also work, but aim for as little air contact as possible. Refrigerate for two days.

Decant the liquid and squeeze the rhubarb to collect any sugar syrup it may have absorbed. Strain the resulting liquid through a fine mesh strainer or coffee filter. The remaining rhubarb can be boiled and puréed, or dehydrated to make candied rhubarb crisp.

Mix the rhubarb syrup with an equal amount of good quality vodka, by weight, to make a liqueur at around 20% abv. Shake gently before use.

Dairy free

INGREDIENTS

Rhubarb and saffron negroni

30ml saffron-infused gin

20ml rhubarb liqueur

15ml Campari

Broad strips of orange peel

Ice

Saffron gin

1 bottle of traditional London Dry-style gin

6–8 threads of saffron

Rhubarb liqueur

Rhubarb stalks

Sugar syrup

Vodka

FALLING WATER

Falling Water is one of the Matterhorn's best-known cocktails. Easy to make, it's the perfect drink for a hot summer's day.

Fill a Collins, highball, or cooler glass with ice and add the feijoa vodka. Slowly top with Ch'i, leaving a wash line about 3cm from the top. Slide a long, diagonally sliced piece of cucumber down the inside of the glass. Depending on its length, it can be useful to try to wrap it in a corkscrew rather than having it protrude. Top up the glass with ice and Ch'i.

Dairy free

INGREDIENTS

30ml 42 Below feijoa vodka

Ch'i herbal mineral water

Cucumber, sliced

Ice

A TASTE OF HISTORY
CUBA STREET HERITAGE BUILDINGS

Much of Cuba Street's character comes from its concentration of late-Victorian and Edwardian-era buildings. Here we've featured 12 of these heritage sites. Next time you wander down the street, be sure to look up! This information is sourced with thanks from the Wellington City Council.

www.wellingtoncityheritage.org.nz

69

CONSTRUCTED 1899
Designed by architect
James O'Dea

The three-storey Royal Oak Hotel is no longer part of the Cuba Street cityscape but there are echoes of its presence in the Oak's complex, on the corner of Cuba and Dixon streets. The original Royal Oak was a popular place to drink in the mid-1800s, until it burned down in 1879 in a fire that saw 30 nearby buildings also destroyed. The last version of the hotel was rebuilt in 1899 and became one of Wellington's most popular fine-dining venues. In the 1930s it was expanded to include accommodation, a dining room and three bars; and from the 1950s the upstairs bar was home to Wellington's LGBT community. It occupied an entire block on Cuba Street until 1981, when it was demolished. From 1888 to 1905, James O'Dea designed over 150 buildings, many of which still stand on Cuba Street today.

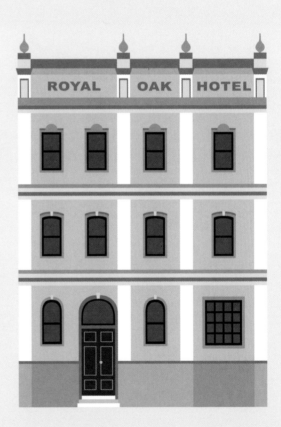

30

CONSTRUCTED 1908

Designed by architect
Joseph McClatchie Dawson

The Columbia Private Hotel opened in January 1909 and remained a private hotel for over 80 years, despite several changes in ownership. It boasted every modern convenience, with over 90 bedrooms, 12 bathrooms, several sitting and writing rooms, and a rooftop garden. It was sold in 1938 and re-opened as Lloyd's Hotel. It made the news in 1940 when a fire broke out on the ground floor and a young waitress perished. From the 1970s the hotel was again known as the Columbia Hotel, before being converted into apartments in the mid-1990s.

118

CONSTRUCTED 1902

Designed by architect
John Swan

The earliest known occupant to fill this narrow commercial building was the Diamond Confectionery Company, which began business there in 1910. In the early 1920s the space was leased to a fruiterer and grocer, Herbert Stanbridge, who occupied it until 1925. Between 1935 and 1995 the premise was occupied by a succession of butchers including the Gear Meat Company Steiner's Butchery, then Cuba Mall Butchery. The butchers shut up shop and were succeeded by the gift store Iko Iko, which opened its doors in 1998 and is still going strong today.

130

CONSTRUCTED 1896

Designed by architect
William Charles Chatfield

The building was constructed for the Gear Meat Preserving and Freezing Company, which occupied it from 1900–1911. Gear Meat Company played a significant role in the early days of the New Zealand meat industry and by the early 1900s was a large exporter of canned and frozen meat. A boot seller converted the space around 1915, and it remained a shoe shop until the late 1920s. In the 1930s it was again a butchery, this time the Manawatu Farmer's Meat Company, but returned to being a shoe shop in the 1940s. Today it's home to STA Travel and a convenience store.

SCOPA CAFFÉ CUCINA

Scopa Caffé Cucina (Scopa) is housed in what used to be Lucky's Corner, an old takeaway and sex shop on a busy corner of Ghuznee and Cuba streets. Although mail still arrives for the sex shop, the site is now a friendly Venetian café, originally set up by brothers Leonardo and Lorenzo with their famous restaurateur father, the late Remiro Bresolin.

For Leonardo and Lorenzo, the world of their childhood was one big playground. They loved mixing with the staff at their father's restaurant, Il Casino. After school they helped out by chopping wood or polishing glasses, and it was great as a kid to be involved. Their father was a playful dad, and made the restaurant business look like fun. The brothers grew up as part of the wider Wellington hospitality family and consider many of their father's peers to be like uncles.

Although the brothers are second-generation restaurateurs and have hospitality in their blood, they've also brought their own ideas about dining to the Wellington scene. Both travelled and worked in Europe before setting up their first business together, Scopa, in 2006.

The brothers really value their staff, nurturing new talent, teaching them skills from scratch, and encouraging them to consider Scopa a second home. And while they continue the tradition of treating staff as family, these days the chef doesn't have a fiery temper and the kitchen is a much calmer place to work! So much so that past staff have gone on to become partners in many of the other businesses the brothers are involved with.

So what is 'scopa' exactly? It's an Italian card game where you sweep up the cards in a winning scoop. The word 'scopa' usually means broom or to sweep, but it also has another meaning – one entirely more adult! It can be met either with indignant outrage or flirty excitement. There has been many an occasion when the Scopa t-shirt has caused a stir. Perhaps echoes of Lucky's Corner sex shop still resonate. But whether it's cards or something a little more risqué, Scopa is a great spot to eat, drink and watch the world go by.

Left: Leonardo and Lorenzo Bresolin

THE CRUST OF LIFE

"It is fair to say that pizza has put a roof over our head.

Our father Remio [Remiro] Bresolin brought pizza to Wellington in the early 1970s, opening La Casa Pizza. We still have our older customers tell us about when they were students and enjoyed the exotic and authentic 'pizza pie' to eat way back then.

Remio then went on to open Il Casino in the late 1970s, which over the years, room by room, grew into the great fine-dining establishment of its 30-year fame. One of the last additions, made in the 1990s, was a wood-fired pizza oven in the restaurant's back courtyard.

Many years later, in 2004, we opened a restaurant, Boulot, on Blair Street, with a wood-fired oven, where our father began to train the next generation of pizza makers.

When the opportunity for the Cuba Street site for Scopa came up, it was a natural progression to follow our pizza roots, and it would be the first time we both went into business together.

Scopa is where Leonardo and I aligned with some clever and passionate people, developing relationships that would grow into great partnerships. Simon Niblett teamed up with us to create the company Dough Holdings. Off the back of Scopa's local success came Duke Carvell's, Crazy Horse – The Steak House, The Gentlemen's Beans Roastery, and Tommy Millions. Tommy was a young financial lawyer who quit his job for the love of dough and to follow his dream of one day opening a New York slice pizza joint. Dough Holdings' greatest venture yet, the Bresolin, opened its doors in 2014 with an eatery that celebrates all things delicious."

Lorenzo Bresolin

Left: Ruben Morfu and Melissa Lombard   Right: Gianluca Cestino

LINGUINE ALLA VONGOLE

We like to use little neck clams from the South Island. They are, however, a bit sandy, as their habitat is in sandy inlets and sheltered harbours. Give these guys a clean under running water but please don't leave them to soak in cold tap water, as this isn't their environment and they will die. Clams have a tendency to open and close – don't be alarmed, it just means they're alive. Find any clams that are not tightly closed, give them a sharp tap and discard any that remain open.

In the restaurant we use fresh pasta, but dry pasta is fine. We recommend the Rustichella brand. It's as good as you would find anywhere in the world – some say it's the best dried pasta anywhere!

Bring a heavy pot of cold, salted water to the boil. The water should be salty like the ocean – you're not going to add any more salt to this dish. Once boiling, add the pasta and stir straight away. It's important to continue stirring until all the pasta is separated. Cook for 12–15 minutes, depending on how al dente you like it.

Heat the olive oil in a large sauté pan, add the garlic, and cook gently for a few minutes until it starts to colour (but don't let it burn or it will taste bitter). Add the chilli and tip in the clams – just add more clams to cater for more friends. Pour in the pinot grigio – and pour a glass for yourself too! Cover the pan with a lid and cook for 60–90 seconds, allowing the clams to open. Discard any clams that don't open.

Add the pasta and parsley to the clams and toss until coated in the sauce. Now serve – and buon appetito!

Serves 4
Dairy free

INGREDIENTS

1kg little neck clams

400g dried pasta

Salt

2 tbsp extra virgin olive oil

3 garlic cloves, finely chopped (Goodfella's style!)

1 red chilli, deseeded and finely chopped

125ml dry white wine; we use a pinot grigio – Enzo's favourite!

1 tbsp Italian parsley, coarsely chopped

POTATO GNOCCHI

Place the potatoes in a large pot and cover with cold water. Bring to the boil, reduce the heat and let simmer for 20–25 minutes or until the potatoes are tender. Drain and mash the potatoes in a large bowl until smooth. Set aside until the mash is cool enough to handle.

Dust the bench with flour. Mix the flour and salt in a small bowl.

Add the egg yolks to the potatoes and stir until combined. Work in the flour then add the grated parmesan. Combine with your hands until the dough starts to clump together. Transfer the dough to the floured surface and knead gently until the dough is smooth and a little sticky.

Be careful not to over-mix or the gnocchi will be tough. Set the dough aside on a well-floured surface and cover with a tea towel.

Tear off a handful of dough and cover the rest so it doesn't dry out. Roll the dough into a 2cm-thick rope and cut into 2cm squares with a sharp knife. Spread the cut gnocchi on a floured surface and sprinkle lightly with flour. Repeat with the rest of the dough.

Bring a large pot of water to the boil and season generously with salt. Drop small amounts of the gnocchi into the boiling water. Once they float to the top, remove with a slotted spoon, refresh in cold water, then drain in a colander. Bring the pot of water back to the boil and repeat until all the gnocchi are poached. Leave them to dry for 15–20 minutes. Keep chilled until ready to use.

The gnocchi is now ready to be pan fried and added to any tomato-based sauce. We serve our gnocchi with Pork and Pancetta Ragù (see page 46).

Serves 8–10
Vegetarian

INGREDIENTS

1½ kg potatoes (agria preferably), peeled and cut into uniform pieces

425g plain flour, sieved

Sea salt flakes

3 egg yolks

200g parmesan, finely grated

Olive oil

PORK AND PANCETTA RAGÙ WITH POTATO GNOCCHI

Heat a heavy pot over a medium heat, adding the oil and vegetables and stirring frequently until the vegetables sweat and appear translucent. When softened, stir through the garlic and chilli flakes. Once everything is translucent and softened, add the dried herbs. These give an intense burst of flavour, which is great in winter.

Finely dice the pancetta, then add to the pot. Fry until soft to release the salty flavour. Add the pork mince while stirring constantly. Once the mince is starting to brown and releasing its juices, add the tomato paste and continue to stir. There's quite a bit of stirring going on now, but you're nearly there! Continue to cook the tomato paste for at least 5–7 minutes over a medium heat while stirring. Be careful not to let the bottom catch. Stir through the tomatoes and simmer for 3–4 hours, the longer the better, over a low heat. Stir sporadically to make sure the bottom isn't catching. After about 3 hours of simmering, season with salt and pepper to taste.

We serve our Pork and Pancetta Ragù over freshly made and pan-fried gnocchi, but it's also great with any other pasta of your choice. If using homemade gnocchi (see page 44), prepare it while the ragù is simmering and keep chilled until ready to serve.

To serve, heat some olive oil in a heavy based frying pan. Once hot, add the gnocchi and gently toss while cooking. Season with salt to taste. When the gnocchi is coloured on all sides, fold through the warm ragù. Serve in your favourite bowls and garnish liberally with parmesan or pecorino cheese, and parsley. Buon appetito!

TIP | This ragù tastes even better the next day, as the flavours will develop overnight.

Serves 8–10

INGREDIENTS

125ml olive oil

1 onion, finely diced

1 carrot, finely diced

3 celery stalks, finely diced

4 garlic cloves, crushed

3 tsp chilli flakes

5 tsp dried basil

5 tsp dried oregano

100g pancetta, finely diced

1kg pork shoulder mince, or any mince with a good amount of fat

200g tomato paste

800g canned whole peeled tomatoes

Sea salt flakes

Freshly ground pepper

To serve

Gnocchi (see page 44)

Shavings of parmesan or pecorino cheese

Fresh parsley, coarsely chopped

146 CUBA STREET
KAFFEE EIS

Karl Tiefenbacher was a foreign-exchange dealer for 18 years before setting up his first Kaffee Eis. The idea of opening a café had always held a nostalgic appeal, with his parents having owned a café during his childhood. So when an opportunity to do the same came up, Karl leapt at the challenge.

Keen to make a career change that made better use of his creative skills, Karl had often discussed with his friends the idea of a takeaway coffee business. So when a friend who'd purchased three shops in Oriental Bay had one become unexpectedly vacant, it was offered to Karl. And so in 2004, Kaffee Eis was born.

The name Kaffee Eis (pronounced café ice), German for 'coffee and ice cream', was chosen to reflect Karl's Austrian heritage. As the café was by the beach, the idea was to sell a bit of ice cream along with the coffee.

A regular trip to Noosa sparked the idea of bringing high-quality gelato to Wellington rather than just selling regular ice cream. From Noosa, Italian contacts were made, machinery sourced, and Kaffee Eis started making gelato. In that first store in Oriental Bay they made the gelato in a tiny space out the back. The freezers generated a lot of heat, resulting in very hot, cramped working conditions, and there wasn't enough space to keep up with the growing demand.

It was a tough nine months, working 14-hour days, seven days a week, before Kaffee Eis opened a factory making Gellicious Gelato. With the factory came the ability to make more gelato, and with more gelato, a need for distribution. The opportunity in 2005 to take over an ice cream shop on the waterfront helped create an even bigger market. Gellicious Gelato is now heading into its second decade, and makes over 40 flavours.

The Cuba Street café opened in November 2013. Leasing the store was a quickly made decision and they opened two weeks later. The company's growth has been fairly organic and now includes five Wellington stores. With over 35 staff, Kaffee Eis often employs students, including Karl's daughter Sarah.

Karl's positivity, energy and ability to act fast have helped build the Kaffee Eis empire. It's hard work, but Karl and partner Jo love what they do. They also like to give back: since October 2016 they've donated 10c from every drink sold. To date they've gifted over $32,000 to a range of local charities.

Left: Jo Healey, Karl and Sarah Tiefenbacher

A DAY IN THE LIFE OF GELLICIOUS GELATO

It all starts in a small factory at the bottom of the Ngaio Gorge, where most days of the week, wearing the attractive get-up of white gumboots and hairnets, Karl and his fellow gelato-maker set about making the day's flavours. With over 40 flavours on the menu, not all of them can be made at once. The day we visited the factory, strawberry, boysenberry and chocolate gelato were in production.

The main thing that strikes you when you see the gelato and sorbet being made is how real it is. The ingredients are very simple and very good. The quality of the chocolate and fresh cream is why the chocolate gelato tastes so luscious. The same goes for the berry flavours. Kilos of perfect fruit are added to the sorbet mix. There's no hiding behind artificial flavours or sub-standard ingredients.

Kaffee Eis gelato is lower in fat than traditional ice cream and has a fuller, more satisfying flavour. The fruit gelato (with the exception of banana) are all sorbetto, which means it's water- rather than milk-based, making it dairy-free, vegan and gluten-free. Made of nearly 40% fresh fruit, it's practically a health food!

Making gelato is surprisingly quick. The ingredients are first heated, then the mixture is transferred to the ice cream machine and rapidly frozen. You can be enjoying a gelato or sorbet within hours of it being made. Yum!

CHOCOLATE BROWNIES

Preheat the oven to 160°C. Line a large baking tin or roasting dish (24 x 34cm) with baking paper. The baking paper should overhang the tin.

Melt the butter in a large bowl, then add the cocoa and beat using an electric mixer. Add the eggs, sugar and vanilla and whizz for 3–4 minutes until the mixture begins to increase in volume to about double. Mix in the chocolate chips/drops. Lastly, stir in the flour and baking powder until fully combined.

Pour the mixture onto the lined baking tin. Gently give it a shake to even out the mixture. Bake for about 1 hour or until an inserted skewer comes out clean. Leave to cool in the tin for about 10 minutes, then turn out onto a wire rack.

When cool, cut into 12–15 squares and sift icing sugar over the top. Serve with a scoop of your favourite ice cream.

Makes 12–15 brownies
Vegetarian

INGREDIENTS

310g butter

1¼ cups cocoa

7 eggs

3 cups sugar

1 tsp vanilla essence

1½ cups good-quality chocolate chips/drops, dark is best

1¼ cups plain flour

1 tsp baking powder

To garnish

Icing sugar

161 CUBA STREET
FLORIDITAS

Julie Clark has always wanted to set up and run a business, and has always naturally gravitated towards food and hospitality. She credits her passion for fresh produce to her grandfather's vegetable garden and the abundant fruit trees on the property where she grew up.

After the success of Clark's Food Merchants, a small deli in Roseneath in the late 1980s, followed by cafés in the Wellington and Palmerston North public libraries (Clark's Library Cafés), Julie and husband James Pedersen were keen to open a bistro-style restaurant. They finally settled on a site in Wellington, originally built in 1912 for a drapery called George and George. They ended up with the site after a laugh over drinks with friends who owned Anise Restaurant. It started with a conversation around the possibility of Anise coming up for sale and Julie jokingly offering $2.50. The Anise owners phoned the next day and said that if she was serious, "lets talk". So they did, and settled on a deal (for somewhat more than the first offer!), opening Floriditas in 2006 in partnership with Marc Weir. Back then, Cuba Street was still a little rough around the edges and it was common for James to walk single women diners to their cars. Since then, they've watched the street develop and grow into the buzzing food district it is today.

While living abroad in the 1980s, Julie honed her cooking skills working at Duff & Trotter and Justin de Blank with the charismatic and talented Gerhard Jenne. She travelled extensively through Europe and Africa encountering a wide range of cuisines and foods, all of which would come to influence the Mediterranean style adopted by Floriditas.

Right: Julie Clark

Finding the very best ingredients is a task Julie takes seriously. Be it investigating roadside stalls or farmers' markets, she goes to great lengths to find the tastiest fruits and vegetables, sourcing produce directly from growers as much as possible. Two of Julie's favourite suppliers are Hawke's Bay-based Bostock Organic Free Range Chicken, and Epicurean Supplies.

BOSTOCK ORGANIC FREE RANGE CHICKEN

Ben and George Bostock grew up on their family's organic apple orchard in Hawke's Bay. They share the family's passion for healthy and safe growing practices, which are controlled from farm to plate. Their orchard also provides the perfect environment for raising chickens. The birds roam freely among the apple trees and are housed in uniquely designed chalets.

EPICUREAN SUPPLIES

Twenty-five years ago, Clyde Potter, owner of Epicurean Supplies, was the first in New Zealand to start growing cavalo nero and Asian greens, as well as other less traditional vegetables. An initial inquiry from a local chef for fresh herbs started this thriving organic business. Today, with a reputation for the rare and unusual, Clyde supplies over 150 different herbs and vegetables to restaurants and stores throughout New Zealand.

SMOKED MACKEREL AND DILL HASH

Fish hash is great for a late breakfast or lunch. In this recipe we use mackerel, but you can use any smoked fish.

Wash the potatoes and boil in salted water until just tender. Be careful not to overcook them – there should be some resistance when you pierce the skin with a sharp knife. Allow the potatoes to cool. This step can be done the night before.

Roughly chop the potatoes into different sizes and keep all the bits of skin on the board (these make the crispy bits). Heat a sturdy frying pan, add the butter and oil and let sizzle. Add the potatoes and cook for approximately 10 minutes, turning occasionally with a fish slice until they're crisp and golden.

Add the smoked fish, dill, parsley, salt and pepper to the pan of potatoes. Flip the mixture a few times to combine, then add two drops of Kaitaia Fire. Bring a small pan of water to a steady simmer. Once the water is simmering, break in the eggs and cook until they are soft-poached (about 3 minutes).

Divide the potato hash onto two warmed plates and top each with a poached egg and a squeeze of lemon juice.

TIP | The key to this recipe is to let the potatoes get brown and crispy.

Serves 2
Gluten free

INGREDIENTS

4 agria potatoes

50g butter

20g olive oil

160g smoked mackerel, broken into flakes

½ cup dill, roughly chopped

½ cup parsley, roughly chopped

Salt

Pepper

2 drops Kaitaia Fire

2 eggs

Lemon wedges

SULTANA AND BUTTERMILK SCONES

Scones are best made and eaten within a couple of hours. The trick to making great scones is cold butter, cold hands, and not too much kneading.

Preheat the oven to 180°C fan forced. Sift the flour, sugar, baking powder and salt into a bowl. With your fingertips, quickly rub the butter into the dry ingredients until completely combined and the mixture looks like fine breadcrumbs. Add the sultanas and toss lightly through the flour mix until coated.

Mix the buttermilk until smooth, then pour it into the flour mixture. Carefully stir to make a soft dough (don't over-mix). Tip the dough onto the bench and gently shape into a 20cm circle. Place a baking tray in the oven to heat up. Cut the dough into 8 equal pieces, like the spokes of a wheel.

Put the scones on the hot tray in a wheel formation with the scones slightly separated. Brush with milk and sprinkle with raw sugar. Bake for 20–25 minutes until golden. Serve warm with butter.

TIP | If you don't have buttermilk you can easily replace it with homemade sour milk. All you need is 1 tablespoon of freshly squeezed lemon juice or white vinegar and 1 cup of milk. Stir together to combine and let sit for 5 minutes, until the milk begins to curdle and becomes acidic.

Makes 8 scones
Vegetarian

INGREDIENTS

450g plain flour

3 tbsp sugar

4½ tsp baking powder

Pinch of salt

100g cold butter

200g sultanas

300ml buttermilk

3 tsp raw sugar

2 tbsp milk, for glazing

170 CUBA STREET
OLIVE

Olive has been a fixture on Cuba Street since 1998. Originally established by Julie Hansen and Karen Krogh, it was named after the large tree in the courtyard. Today, Olive is owned by brothers Ferdi and Carlo Petagna, and executive chef Jamie Morgan.

Having previously worked together, Jamie and Ferdi were keen to set up a restaurant in Wellington. In 2014 they had the opportunity to take over Olive – just one week before Christmas!

After spending 13 years overseas developing his skills as a chef, Jamie returned to Wellington in pursuit of a change of pace, a commitment to family, and a desire to challenge himself by being a business owner. At Olive, with around 27 staff, it's a busy life, but being back in Wellington and working on Cuba Street make the hard work worth it. Jamie enjoys the challenge of making stuff happen, and even if change can sometimes be slow, the results are always rewarding.

Ferdi's career began as a marketing student working in restaurants, where he discovered a passion for the business. As well as managing Olive, he's in charge of keeping the courtyard looking good. He's discovered he has surprisingly green thumbs – and an expensive passion for palms!

So what's good at Olive? The Wednesday waffle special has proved a hit, with the chef shaking up variants on the classic theme. Like many of the cafés on Cuba Street, brunch is always busy. But at Olive, a flair for creating innovative dishes using fresh local produce really showcases the talents of Jamie and his staff.

Right: Jamie Morgan

AWATORU

Olive has a history of taking care over the produce they use, and part of that commitment is evident in their patronage of wild-food supplier, Awatoru. The produce is harvested in a sustainable manner, and its freshness all the way to the plate makes this a perfect partnership.

Scott and Maaike McNeil are Awatoru ('three rivers'), a small fishing and wild-food business based on the Kapiti coast. About nine years ago the couple moved to Waikanae with a small fishing boat, wanting to make a living out of Scott's passion for hunting and fishing.

They spent the first five years catching paddle crabs and diversified from there to make the business sustainable all year round. Today, albacore tuna is their main catch. They spend four months of the year fishing for tuna, and the rest smoking and processing it into pastrami and other products. They also source other sustainably harvested wild foods from around New Zealand, including venison and scallops. A good reputation and word of mouth have helped their business grow.

Scott and Maaike love to be involved in all aspects of the business, dealing with fishermen and hunters as well as with chefs. At times it has been helpful to educate chefs about fresh and sustainable fishing, and in turn Awatoru have learned how chefs like to have their produce supplied or prepared. They've found that the more involved you are in the supply chain, the better the understanding all round.

Awatoru is a family business, although Maaike struggles at time with its more brutal aspects: she's been known to rescue a beached bream and shed a tear or two over a deer!

Left: Scott McNeil

SCALLOPS WITH PARMESAN AND BLACK PEPPER FARROTTO

This dish is delicious at lunchtime with a glass of viognier or rosé. We use Bream Bay scallops (DOC approved), supplied to us by Scott from Awatoru. You can substitute the scallops for prawns or halloumi and basil.

FARROTTO | Soak the farro overnight to soften it. We like to soak our farro in the whey left over from making ricotta. Place the soaked farro in a saucepan with the stock so that it is covered. Cook over a medium-high heat, bringing it to the boil and simmering for about 15 minutes (when cooked, farro should be a bit firm to the bite). Drain and reserve the stock. Put the cooked farro and 75ml of the reserved stock back into the saucepan over a low heat. Add the parmesan, pepper and chives, and stir until a risotto-like consistency has been achieved. Juice the lemon and add with the butter to the farrotto. Salt to taste.

SCALLOPS | Melt the butter in a saucepan over a medium heat. Fry the scallops for 2 minutes, flipping once, until golden brown on both sides but still soft on the inside.

TO SERVE | Dish a good helping of farrotto into a bowl and garnish with the scallops, a little grated parmesan, snow pea tendrils and a wedge of lemon. Serve with a fresh leafy salad and crusty bread.

Serves 4–6
Vegetarian option

INGREDIENTS

Farrotto

2 cups farro

1.5 litres vegetable stock

½ cup Grana Padano or Gran Moravia cheese, grated

A few good grinds of cracked pepper

1 small handful chopped chives

1–2 knobs of butter

Salt

½ lemon

Scallops

1 tbsp butter

350–400g scallops (with roe)

Garnish

Lemon wedges

Snow pea tendrils

OLIVE

SALTED CARAMEL AND BANANA WAFFLES

This dish is a brunch-time favourite at Olive. The waffles are airy, delicious and sweet, with a touch of saltiness. We use a waffle iron to cook them, but don't despair if you don't have one – this batter doubles as a pancake mixture!

WAFFLE BATTER | Heat the waffle iron if you have one. Whisk the egg whites until they form firm peaks and leave to one side while you mix the flour, baking powder and sugar in a separate, large bowl. Add the vanilla essence, milk and yolks to the dry ingredients, and mix to combine. Fold in the melted butter and lastly the egg whites.

When the waffle iron is ready, use a ladle to pour in portions of batter. This recipe makes approximately 15 waffles.

SALTED CARAMEL | Heat the water in a small saucepan over a high heat and pour in the sugar. Bring to the boil and cook 3–4 minutes, until the sugar has dissolved and the syrup is golden (you shouldn't need to stir it). Take the saucepan off the heat and whisk in the cream, butter and salt until thick and shiny.

TO SERVE | Cut the waffles into triangles and arrange them on plates. Place sliced banana over the waffles, drizzle with salted caramel sauce, and sprinkle with grated chocolate to finish.

Serves 4–6
Vegetarian

INGREDIENTS

Waffle batter

2¼ cups flour

2½ tsp baking powder

4 tbsp sugar

1 tbsp vanilla essence

325ml milk

4 eggs, whites only

120g butter, melted

30g cooking oil

Salted caramel

80ml water

1¼ cups sugar

120ml cream

25g butter

¼ tsp salt

Garnish

2 bananas, sliced

Dark chocolate, grated

MIDNIGHT ESPRESSO

Midnight Espresso was opened in 1989 by primary-school friends Geoff Marsland and Tim Rose. On a trip to Vancouver they discovered Joe's Café, a popular joint filled with great vibes, coffee and music. The two friends found something at Joe's they wanted to bring back to Wellington.

After tracking down and shipping a commercial espresso machine to Wellington, Geoff and Tim took over the site of a greasy spoon called The Hob, in the old Watkins building on Cuba Street. The café was narrow and dark, and the street was definitely seedy, but they saw the potential in the space and the location. After 10 days of frenzied renovation and with help from friends, the café opened.

It was officially named Havana Midnight Espresso, a compromise between Tim's idea of talking to the Cuban name of the street and Geoff's description of what the café was about – late night coffee. Today it's simply known as Midnight Espresso.

Midnight Espresso was a place to go late at night where you didn't have to buy alcohol. Liquor licensing was tricky back in the 1980s, and not serving it meant they could stay open for as long as they liked. It soon became a popular destination for artists, sex workers, students, office workers, police, ambulance drivers, and many other weird and wonderful Wellingtonians.

Geoff and Tim eventually began to import and roast coffee beans, and later moved on from Midnight Espresso, selling the café to another of Geoff's primary-school mates, Hamish McIntyre. Hamish was looking for something new and admits he never really thought too hard about taking over Midnight Espresso, he just did it. His motto was: if it worked do it; if not, don't.

Hamish hasn't changed much about Midnight Espresso since taking it over nearly 20 years ago, and many of its original customers are still regulars. It has remained so true to its roots that some people are convinced Hamish is, in fact, the well-known coffee baron Geoff Marsland. Hamish doesn't often correct them when they mistake him for the original owner. Geoff is still a regular at Midnight Espresso, popping in most mornings for breakfast.

Hamish's four daughters are a big part of his life. The two eldest, Shinee and Zara, split their time between their own business, Half Baked Catering Co., and working at Midnight Espresso, helping manage the kitchen and the baking.

Right: Zara, Hamish and Shinee McIntyre

178 CUBA
Midnight Espresso
WE SELL
HAVANA
COFFEE
BEANS
Midnight Espresso
OPEN
363 DAYS OF THE YEAR
7:30 AM to 3 AM
WEEKDAYS
8 AM to 3 AM
WEEKENDS
and
PUBLIC HOLIDAYS
ZEUS
ISLAND BAY BUTCHERY
STOP FACTORY FARMING

HAVANA COFFEE WORKS

Havana Coffee Works has played a huge part in the evolution of great coffee in New Zealand. Sourcing green beans from Cuba and worldwide, their single origin and special-blend hot air roasted coffees are popular as well as ethical.

After setting up Midnight Espresso, Geoff Marsland and Tim Rose opened Deluxe, a little café next to the Embassy Theatre. Both cafés were successful – and getting through a lot of coffee. The desire to control the flavour of the coffee and satisfy the growing demands of their cafés propelled them in the direction of roasting their own beans – not an easy task in 1990.

Inspired by new roasting methods used in Europe and helped by inventor Russell Collins, their first hot air roaster was made, lovingly named the Voltair Type 1, and put to work in a room above Midnight Espresso on Cuba Street. The roaster was definitely an example of Kiwi ingenuity and was a little rudimentary, but it was the start of a new way of roasting beans in New Zealand. When the Voltair caused a fire, Havana Coffee Works was kicked out of the Watkins building. The need for new premises and a new roaster saw them shift to Wigan Street in 1992, setting up in an old workman's cottage once reputed to be an opium den and now the site of Havana Bar.

The next step was to source their own beans. Motivated to find the best beans in the world, they founded Coffee Imports in 1997. On a trip to Jamaica they glimpsed the island of Cuba in the distance and wanted to know what the coffee was like there. With a café on Cuba Street and a roasting business called Havana, sourcing beans from Cuba would, of course, be perfect.

Once the importing side of the business took over they decided to give up the cafés. In 2008 they moved to new premises on Tory Street, to what has to be the coolest coffee roasting factory/café/lab ever. Today they import coffee beans from 14 countries, roasting about 400 tonnes a year – enough to make around 380,000 cups of coffee a week!

Left: Joe Stoddart   Right: Geoff Marsland

MOUSETRAPS

Mousetraps have always been on the menu at Midnight Espresso. This variation on a Kiwi classic is perfect for an easy anytime snack.

Preheat the oven to 180°C. Line a baking tray with baking paper and lay the slices of bread on it. Spread the relish on the bread and sprinkle over some grated cheese. On two of the slices, place 3 asparagus spears and 3 strips of red pepper. Slice the marinated or cooked mushrooms and place on the other two pieces of bread. Sprinkle parmesan on all of the slices to taste, and bake for 15 minutes until golden brown. Serve immediately.

Serves 2
Vegetarian

INGREDIENTS

4 slices Vogel's bread

4 tsp tomato relish

1½ cups cheese, grated

3 asparagus spears, tinned or fresh

Roasted red pepper strips

3–4 portobello mushrooms, marinated or stir-fried

Parmesan, finely grated

GLUTEN-FREE CARROT CAKE

Preheat the oven to 180°C. Grease a 21cm round cake tin and put aside.

Put all the cake ingredients in a large bowl and mix together with a spoon. Pour the mixture into the cake tin and bake for approximately 30–35 minutes, until the cake is golden brown and bounces back to the touch. Allow it to cool in the tin.

This carrot cake is delicious on its own but is also very nice with cream cheese icing. To make the icing, place all the ingredients in a food processor and blend until whipped.

To make a layered cake, make two cakes and spread the icing between the layers.

TIP | This recipe can be used to make muffins instead of a whole cake. Pour the mixture into a greased muffin tin and bake for approximately 20 minutes.

Makes 1 cake or 12 muffins
Gluten free, vegetarian

INGREDIENTS

¾ cup chopped walnuts

2 cups grated carrot

1¼ cups rice flour

1 tsp mixed spice

½ tsp ginger

½ tsp cinnamon

1 tsp baking soda

1 tsp baking powder

1 cup soft brown sugar

3 eggs

1 cup canola oil

1 tsp vanilla essence

½ cup sultanas

2 tbsp desiccated coconut

Cream cheese icing (optional)

4 tbsp cream cheese

2 tbsp butter

2 cups icing sugar

1 tsp vanilla essence

MIDNIGHT ESPRESSO | 77

HALF BAKED CATERING CO.

It's not surprising that sisters Shinee and Zara are good at baking – as the daughters of Midnight Espresso's Hamish McIntyre, they practically grew up in the kitchen.

Working at Midnight Espresso was an invaluable way to learn how to make wholesome food, and gave Shinee and Zara the chance to experiment with recipes. More recently they've stepped out on their own with the Half Baked Catering Co., specialising in raw, healthy sweet treats. Their journey into raw food was largely influenced by their mother having coeliac disease and the desire to cut sugar from their own diets. Seeing the raw food movement grow internationally, they saw space in Wellington to develop their company.

It's been hard graft, often working all day at Midnight Espresso and baking late into the night for Half Baked, but they love the creativity that comes with doing their own thing. They've been amazed by the positive response to their food. With the business quickly growing, they've had to cut back on working at Midnight Espresso, freeing them up to develop more of their vegan and gluten-free treats. Their latest venture has been designing the packaging for their Maui Wowee and Snicky Fingers bars.

Running a business is still pretty new and the sisters have had a lot to learn. When they first started in January 2016 they were grateful for the support of David Nalder at Moore Wilson's, who stocked their products and offered valuable business advice along the way. They've gone from having a small selection in the cake cabinet to a nice large one, with their products often outselling the more traditional bakery offerings. Most of their cakes are a great option for people with dietary issues, but best of all they look and taste amazing!

Right: Zara and Shinee McIntyre

SUPERFOOD BALLS

In a large mixing bowl, combine the ground almonds, nuts, seeds, salt, vanilla, coconut oil, apricot pieces, and orange zest and juice. Mix together with a spoon, then add the date paste. Keep mixing until the mixture has a wet but firm consistency.

Place the desiccated coconut on a plate or in a wide bowl. Use your hands to form the mixture into balls, then roll each ball in the coconut until covered. Store in the fridge in an airtight container.

TIP | Lightly roasting the nuts and seeds before adding them to the mixture will give the superfood balls a stronger, nuttier flavour.

Makes 12
Gluten free, raw, vegan

INGREDIENTS

1 cup ground almonds

½ cup chopped almonds

½ cup chopped walnuts

½ cup sunflower seeds

½ cup pumpkin seeds

½ tsp Himalayan salt

½ tsp vanilla essence

¼ cup melted coconut oil

½ cup dried apricot, chopped

1 orange, zest and juice

¼ – ½ cup date paste

½ cup desiccated coconut

181 CUBA STREET
LORETTA

Loretta is the restaurant that owner and chef Marc Weir has been dreaming of since starting out in restaurants in his early twenties.

Loretta was set up in 2014 in anticipation of the lease expiring on Floriditas, the Cuba Street restaurant jointly owned by Marc Weir, Julie Clark and James Pedersen. But a new landlord, earthquake strengthening, and the lease's renewal meant they ended up with two busy restaurants instead of one. To make the most of both, Marc took over the running and ownership of Loretta, while Julie now runs and owns Floriditas with James.

The interior of Loretta is a real surprise. Its subtle street presence makes it easy to miss, but it's a lot bigger on the inside – seating up to 120 people and extending all the way back to Swan Lane, it seems to go on forever! Originally built in 1916 as a pharmacy and one of Wellington's first cinemas, the Queen's Picture Theatre, today's award-winning interior is sensitive to much of the building's original structure. Marc's involvement with the design is evident, and the decor includes various items he's collected over the years in anticipation of Loretta happening one day.

Loretta is busiest at the weekend, often serving 700 brunches a day and sometimes as many as 1,000. The cuisine is simple and predominantly plant-based, with the use of plenty of fresh herbs. The menu reflects Marc's lifelong passion for fresh, whole food. The cakes and sweet treats are from the Ugly Duck Bakery, co-owned with Julie Clark. The beautiful food plus the regular positioning of rustic bowls of fruit and vegetables, flowers, fresh bread and preserves, make this restaurant feel like a contemporary still-life painting.

Left: Marc Weir

192 CUBA STREET
LOGAN BROWN

When you first walk into Logan Brown it's hard not to be impressed. Behind the big red doors on the corner of Cuba and Vivian streets is one of New Zealand's best-known restaurants, housed in one of Wellington's most imposing heritage buildings.

Originally set up in 1996 by restaurateur Steve Logan and chef Al Brown, today Logan Brown is a partnership between chef Shaun Clouston, Debbie Jones and Steve Logan. Logan Brown is a beautiful restaurant, but the place is more than good looks and fine dining. At its heart are three important principles: kia ora, kai, and kaitiaki. Kia ora is a friendly welcome; kai is the connection to where our food comes from and how it's prepared; and kaitiaki is all about community.

Kia ora is a genuine Kiwi welcome! Behind the red doors there's always a warm greeting and friendly service. Logan Brown has become an internationally recognised destination for people wanting to experience the best of Kiwi hospitality and cuisine.

Shaun and Steve are passionate about kai, and feel fortunate to be so close to the source of this country's best ingredients. For over 20 years they've built strong relationships with the New Zealanders who grow, farm and catch some of our best produce. Their commitment to these suppliers is a big part of the Logan Brown story.

Right: Debbie Jones and Steve Logan

At Logan Brown, kaitiaki is about taking care of the environment and nurturing community. They serve only sustainably and ethically sourced produce. Shaun's passion for sustainable fishing was further encouraged by his young daughter when she learned about the overfishing of whitebait. Now, endangered seafood is never on Logan Brown's menu, and Shaun hopes that if more restaurants did the same it would reduce the numbers fished.

Shaun and Steve's energy for community involvement and collaboration is inspiring. They play an active part in the Cuba Street neighbourhood by encouraging and supporting its businesses. They were the Cuba Fruit Mart's first wholesale customer – a relationship fuelled by many a tasty Indian barbecue! They also give back to the community more widely. Logan Brown is involved in an array of conservation initiatives, including the Garden to Table programme for primary-school children, which promotes growing and cooking food from scratch. Shaun and Steve can sometimes be found demonstrating to children that preparing even the simplest of meals is a great way to show friends and family your love.

BRAISED BEEF SHORT RIB

SHORT RIB | Seal the beef ribs, then place in an ovenproof dish. Preheat the oven to 165°C. Heat the hoisin, spices and liquids together, and pour over the beef ribs. Cover the dish and place in the oven. Braise slowly until tender, approximately 2½ hours, then allow the ribs to cool properly in the liquid. Heat to serve.

SHALLOT CRUNCHINESS | Peel and slice shallots into rings 3–4mm thick and soak in water overnight. The next day, rinse and dry. Heat some sunflower oil in a deep pot heated to 150°C, add the shallots in batches, and turn the heat down low. Cook long and slow for an hour, or until the bubbles stop. Bring back up to a high heat, stirring continuously, until golden. Drain and place on a paper towel to absorb any excess oil. Serve on top of the cooked short ribs.

SAFFRON PICKLED ONIONS | Peel the pickling onions, cut in half lengthways and separate into individual cups. Toast saffron lightly in a pan (be careful, it burns easily). Combine saffron, water and vinegar in a pot and bring to the boil. Pour the saffron pickle over the raw onion cups and place a cartouche (paper cover) over the onions to ensure they're submerged in liquid. Seal the container and leave the onions to steep.

CARAMELIZED ONIONS | Peel the onions, trimming out as much of the core as possible, then French-cut them – cut in half then slice lengthways. Place into a pot, add the salt and mix well. Cook on a low heat and stir often until the onions are evenly brown, for approximately 2 hours.

The recipe continues on the next page.

Serves 6

INGREDIENTS

Short rib

2kg beef short rib

120g hoisin sauce

50g fresh ginger

4 garlic cloves

2 star anise, whole

10 cloves, whole

½ tsp Szechuan peppercorns

160ml pale ale

80ml mirin

70ml soy sauce

600ml chicken stock

Shallot crunchiness

300g banana shallots

Saffron pickled onions

200g pickling onions

1 pinch saffron threads

300ml white vinegar

300ml water

Salt

Caramelized onions

500g brown onions

½ teaspoon sea salt flakes

CONFIT WAGYU ONIONS | Peel the onions and leave them whole, then heat enough wagyu fat to cover the onions. Add the onions to the fat and confit until soft, cooking them a little further but being careful not to over-cook. Remove the onions and leave to cool. To serve, cut in half and char, then season to taste.

SMOKED CARROT PURÉE | Peel the carrots and slice as mirepoix, then hot smoke for 10 minutes. Season with salt and olive oil, then cover with baking paper and a lid. Cook at 160°C until very tender. Place in a blender and blend until smooth. Add water if needed to achieve purée consistency. Pass through the finest sieve and adjust seasoning to taste.

SLOW-ROASTED CARROTS | Scrub the carrots clean, leaving skins on and trimming away 95% of the green stem from the carrot top. Place in a grilling pan on a low heat and brush with clarified butter, turning every 2 minutes until cooked.

GARNISH | Slice carrots into ice water using a truffle slicer. To serve, place on a paper towel and season. Forage nasturtium leaves, wash and cut to size using a cutter ring. Store in a plastic box with damp paper towels until ready to serve.

TO SERVE | Serve each beef short rib topped with crisp shallots accompanied with the saffron pickled onions, caramelized onion, confit wagyu onions, smoked carrot purée and slow-roasted carrots. Decorate the dish with the garnish.

Confit wagyu onions
200g pickling onions
Wagyu fat

Smoked carrot purée
200g carrots
Olive oil
Salt
Water

Slow-roasted carrots
12 baby carrots
Clarified butter

Garnish
Raw baby carrot slices
Nasturtium leaves

RABBIT AND PORK RILLETTES

RILLETTES | Marinate the pork with salt, pepper, sugar, juniper and rosemary for 2 days. Mix the remaining ingredients with the pork and cook at 150°C for 4–5 hours – the longer the better. Leave to cool, then refrigerate overnight. Melt the fat and then pick out the meat. For the rabbit, bring all ingredients to the boil except the rabbit legs, ice and pink salt. Take off the heat and add the ice. Once cold, add the pink salt and rabbit legs. Marinate for 2 days. Wash off the brine before covering and confit in duck fat at 150°C for 1½–2 hours. Let chill. Pick the confit rabbit and add to the pork. Mix and season. Place in a cylinder mould to shape, leaving a gap for the duck fat, then chill. Pour ½ tablespoon of melted duck fat on top and leave to set.

ROSEMARY LAVOSH | Sieve the dry ingredients together and add the rosemary. Whisk together the oil and water. Add the wet ingredients to the dry ingredients and mix to a dough. Knead lightly and let rest in the fridge overnight. Roll the dough thinly using a pasta machine and place on oiled baking trays. Brush with oil and salt flakes. Bake at 170°C for 10 minutes.

CRANBERRY AND APPLE RELISH | It's important to have all the ingredients ready before making this relish. In a large pot, add the sugar and water and cook to a golden caramel. Add zest and ginger and cook for approximately 10 seconds, then add the orange juice to 'stop cooking'. Add cranberries and cook out until they are starting to break down and the relish thickens. Add apples and cook for 15 minutes. Add white pepper to taste.

WALNUT MUSTARD | Toast the walnuts in the oven at 160°C until evenly coloured. Set aside to cool. Once cool, chop and mix with the mustard and shallots. Season with sherry vinegar and salt.

APPLE JELLY | Place the gelatine into iced water to bloom. Gently reduce the vinegar until almost evaporated. Add the juice and reduce to 250ml. Add the gelatine and calvados, mix well and refrigerate until it sets. Dice just before serving, plating with the rillettes, mustard, garnish, lavosh and relish.

Serves 6
Dairy free

INGREDIENTS

Rillettes – pork

200g wild pork shoulder, diced largely

100g pork back fat

100g pork belly, skin removed

10g sea salt

3g white pepper, ground

5g sugar

5g juniper, ground

2g rosemary, finely chopped

½ onion, studded with cloves

½ carrot, cut lengthways

1 bay leaf

2 peppercorns, whole

Thyme

Rillettes – rabbit

600g rabbit legs, bone in

80g duck fat

½ cup sea salt flakes

2 tbsp garlic, minced

1 tbsp peppercorns, milled

½ tbsp juniper berries

½ cup sugar

2 dry bay leaves

⅓ tsp pink salt

¼ bunch thyme

230ml water

260g ice

INGREDIENTS

Rosemary lavosh

2 ½ cups plain flour

2 tsp fine salt

2 tbsp rosemary, chopped

1 cup water

½ cup olive oil

Cranberry and apple relish

200g sugar

80ml water

1 ½ oranges, zest and juice

30g ginger, peeled and finely chopped

1kg cranberries

2 granny smith apples, peeled and diced 1cm

¼ tsp white pepper, ground

Walnut mustard

3 tbsp walnuts

3 tbsp wholegrain mustard

½ tsp shallots, finely chopped

Sherry vinegar to taste

Apple jelly

3 ½ gelatine leaves

Iced water

100ml cider vinegar

1 litre apple juice

1 tbsp calvados

Pickles and watercress, to garnish

DARK CHOCOLATE CRÉMEUX

CHOCOLATE CRÉMEUX | Combine the cream and milk in a pot and bring to a simmer. In a separate bowl, blend the eggs using a stick blender. Slowly pour a third of the warm cream mix into the eggs while still blending, then pour back into the rest of the cream and gently heat to 80°C. Remove from the heat and add the chocolate, stirring until the chocolate is melted, then use the stick blender again to fully combine the mix. Pass the mixture through a fine sieve, then pour either into single moulds or a tray for portioning later.

BALSAMIC POACHED CHERRIES | Combine all ingredients apart from the cherries in a pot. Bring the mixture to the boil, then reduce the heat and simmer for a couple of minutes. Put the cherries in a separate container and pour the hot liquid over the top. Cover with a piece of baking paper and allow to cool. Reserve the liquid for later.

BALSAMIC CHERRY GEL | In a small saucepan, whisk together the liquid and agar. Bring to a simmer, whisking continuously. Allow to simmer for 1 minute, then pour the mixture into a bowl or container. Put in the fridge until completely cool and has set, then blend with a stick blender until smooth. Pass the gel through a fine sieve.

RASPBERRY-DUSTED MERINGUE KISSES | Whisk the egg whites using a kitchen mixer on medium speed until foamy, then slowly pour in the sugar while slightly increasing the mixer's speed. Beat until stiff peaks form. Put meringue mixture into a piping bag with a small nozzle and pipe little 'kisses' onto lined baking trays. Using a small sieve, gently dust with the freeze-dried raspberry powder. Allow to dry overnight in an oven at 50°C, or in a dehydrator.

The recipe continues on the next page.

Serves 6

INGREDIENTS

Chocolate crémeux

375ml cream

140ml milk

2 eggs

350g dark chocolate

Balsamic poached cherries

250g sugar

175ml balsamic vinegar

150ml red wine

150ml orange juice

1 sprig fresh tarragon

1 tbsp black peppercorns, whole

500g fresh cherries

Balsamic cherry gel

330ml cherry poaching liquid

3g agar

Raspberry-dusted meringue kisses

100g egg whites, room temperature

190g sugar

1 tbsp freeze-dried raspberry powder

HOKEY POKEY | Stir to combine the sugar, honey, glucose and water in a stainless-steel pot. Place on a medium heat and bring to the boil. Continue to boil until the sugar reaches 153–160°C. Remove from the heat and use a whisk to quickly beat in the baking soda. Immediately pour the hokey pokey onto a lined baking tray and allow to cool.

CHOCOLATE MACARONS | Sieve the icing sugar, ground almonds and cocoa together through a fine-meshed sieve, making sure they are well combined. Put the egg whites in a very clean metal mixing bowl. Whisk on medium speed to a soft foam. Turn up the speed slightly and slowly pour in the caster sugar. Beat until stiff and glossy. Using a spatula, gently fold in the almond mix one-third at a time. Fold until the mixture runs smoothly from the spatula but still holds soft peaks for a short time.

Pour into a piping bag with a 1cm nozzle. Hold the nozzle slightly above a tray lined with a silicon mat or baking paper, and pipe into even circles. Once the tray is full, tap it gently on the bench to remove any air bubbles. Allow the macarons to sit for around 30 minutes or until they have dried slightly on the outside – this will help them rise evenly.

Bake at 130°C for 14 minutes. Allow to cool on the tray, and then arrange the macarons in pairs of the same size. Fill with chocolate buttercream using the same nozzle. Don't fill to the edges; instead, gently push the two halves together to spread the icing to the edges.

CHOCOLATE BUTTERCREAM | In a kitchen mixer, beat the butter until light and creamy. Add the icing sugar in about four additions, starting on a low speed and scraping down the sides of the bowl after each addition. Add the cocoa and beat until well combined.

TO SERVE | Serve the chocolate crémeux with poached cherries, cherry gel, hokey pokey, meringues and macarons. Garnish the dish with freeze-dried raspberries.

Hokey pokey

160g sugar

25g honey

62g glucose

2 tbsp water

7g baking soda

Chocolate macarons

140g egg whites, room temperature

215g caster sugar

115g icing sugar

100g ground almonds

15g high-quality cocoa

Chocolate buttercream

150g butter, softened

250g icing sugar

40g cocoa

Garnish

Freeze-dried raspberries, powdered and whole

CUBA FRUIT MART

The Cuba Fruit Mart and the family of Dayal Makan have been present on Cuba Street since 1964. The Fruit Mart is still in the family and is now run by Sanjay Dayal and his sister Joshna, who took over from their father Magan and uncles Lucky and Wally.

For Sanjay, ending up at the Fruit Mart just happened. He already had a commerce degree, but a casual offer to help his dad turned into much more: it felt good to be working with family, and being young and fit meant he could do the heavy lifting.

In the early days the wholesale side of the business was a little basic. They made deliveries by car, which meant having to go back to the shop frequently to load the next order. Then Sanjay meet Logan Brown's original owners Steve Logan and Al Brown. As the story goes, Al was drawn to the Fruit Mart by the delicious aroma of an Indian lunch Sanjay's mum had cooked. He came in to enquire about the food, and from there persuaded Sanjay to supply produce to Logan Brown wholesale. At first Sanjay was intimidated by the size of the challenge, but today the Fruit Mart is wholesaler to a number of Wellington restaurants, many of them on Cuba Street.

The business has grown sixfold since Sanjay and Joshna took over, and while things are run a little differently than before, it's still very much a family concern. What Sanjay loves about his job is taking a punt on a new product and seeing chefs pick it up and do amazing things with it. He also gets to make friends with many of the others who work on Cuba Street. The only things he finds frustrating are the seven-day working weeks and early-morning starts. But as long as his customers are happy and he still gets to go fishing sometimes, it's all good!

Left: Wally Dayal, Sanjay and Joshna Dayal   Right: Sanjay Dayal and Jamie Morgan

MASALA SPICED BARBECUE LAMB CHOPS

This is a recipe our extended family has used for as long as I [Sanjay] can remember. It is a mainstay at any BBQ or Christmas lunch. The masala marinade works best with lamb chops but can also be used with chicken or fish. Every family has their own take on this recipe – just adjust the spices to suit your taste.

Combine all the paste ingredients in a large bowl, then add the lamb. Massage the masala paste into the chops to cover as evenly as possible. Cover the bowl with cling film or store in an airtight container. For best results, allow to marinate for 1–2 days in the fridge. If you choose to barbecue the chops straight away they won't be as tender and flavoursome as after a couple of days of marinating.

Oil the grill or cooking surface to avoid sticking. Barbecue the chops over charcoal or gas (we only ever use charcoal) at a medium to high heat until cooked to your liking (we cook them medium-rare). The cooking time varies depending on the size of the chops.

Serve the lamb chops straight from the grill, topped with more lemon juice and chopped coriander.

Serves 8–10
Dairy free, gluten free

INGREDIENTS

2kg lamb forequarter chops

Masala paste

2 tsp garam masala

3 tsp ground coriander seeds

2 tsp ground cumin seeds

3–4 fresh chillies, finely chopped (adjust to suit your taste – the hotter the chops, the more beer you will drink!)

1 tbsp garlic, finely chopped

1 tbsp fresh ginger, finely chopped

2 tsp of salt

3 tbsp lemon juice, freshly squeezed

¼ cup fresh coriander leaves, chopped

¼ cup canola oil

To serve

Lemon juice

Fresh coriander, roughly chopped

EL MATADOR

Established in 2012 by classically trained chef Mike Marsland, El Matador feels a lot like an authentic side-street eatery in Buenos Aires. A bold move by someone who has never been to Argentina!

After wrapping up Ernesto café further down Cuba Street, in a building vacated for earthquake strengthening, Mike was looking to set up a new restaurant. He thought of expanding on the Cuban theme by looking to Che Guevara, the Argentinian revolutionary who was a major player in the Cuban revolution. Mike was also drawn to the Argentinian passion for barbecued meat, loving the drama and flavour of food cooked on a real wood-fired grill. The Argentinian asado (barbecue) would be a real point of difference for this chef used to cooking fine French cuisine.

Fitted-out to feel like an old Buenos Aires eatery and bar, El Matador is deliberately rustic, down to the original tiles from the restaurant's previous life as a butchery – a fabulous connection for a restaurant largely about meat.

Mike Marsland is one of Cuba Street's longest-serving chefs and restaurateurs. His career began in the kitchen at Le Normandie, one of Wellington's finest French restaurants, also on Cuba Street. Set up by Renée Louise Charlton, also known as Madame Louise, Le Normandie brought French cuisine and fine dining to the capital in the 1960s and 1970s.

Mike went on to study, then moved quickly up the ranks in a number of Wellington restaurants; at just 23 he was head chef at Plimmer restaurant. At that time, in the 1980s, the Wellington restaurant scene was young and heavily influenced by classical French cooking. Tiring of working for the top end of restaurants as an employee, Mike craved the chance to set up his own business. When brother Geoff came back from overseas with an espresso machine and set up Midnight Espresso, Mike was inspired to do his own thing too. With help from his brother, he opened Espressoholic on Willis Street in 1989. He went on to have two other popular cafés, both on Cuba Street – Krazy Lounge and Ernesto. Today, he owns El Matador along with Ekim, the burger truck near the top of Cuba Street.

Right: Mike Marsland

The restaurant business can be hard work and there's often a fine line between financial success and failure. When asked why he does it, Mike is nothing but pragmatic: "This is what I do. When you know you are the one responsible for creating this place with happy diners and great food it's very rewarding. The hardest thing is the clock on the wall – turning food around quickly can at times be very stressful."

These days Mike focuses more on spending time with his kids. With long and often unsociable hours, the hospitality business can be hard on families. Having created the culture of El Matador, he lets his staff take on more of the work, preferring not to work nights so he can be at home with his family. In the mornings, however, he can still be found in the restaurant making bread and preparing for the day ahead. It's impressive watching Mike whip up burger buns, ciabatta and fugazza, while answering the phone and talking to suppliers who come in with various produce, as well as anyone else who pops in for a hello and a chat. This is a man who can multi-task!

One of Mike's regular visitors is long-time Cuba Street tailor, Loukas Hazitzi. Loukas started working on the street in 1967, when part of his job was fitting Air New Zealand hostesses with uniforms. Loukas isn't quite ready to retire yet – being on Cuba Street is a hard habit to break – and he still works a few hours every day. He loves to pop into El Matador for a chat while Mike makes the bread, and often scores a free loaf of fresh ciabatta.

Right: Loukas Hazitzi

CHIMICHURRI

Chimichurri is to Argentinians what tomato sauce on sausages is to Kiwis. In Argentina, whether you're at a gaucho campfire or society wedding, you'll always find chimichurri.

Put the crushed garlic, chopped herbs, red capsicum and onion into a bowl. Add the remaining ingredients and whisk together. Cover and refrigerate for at least 2 hours up to a day to allow the flavours to meld.

Serve the chimichurri on top of the Parrilla Grilled Beef Short Rib (see page 106) or with any barbecued meats, fish and vegetables.

Store chimichurri in an airtight container in the fridge for up to two weeks.

Makes 4 cups
Gluten free, vegan

INGREDIENTS

6 garlic cloves, crushed

3 cups flat-leaf parsley, finely chopped

2 cups oregano leaves, finely chopped

1 red capsicum, finely chopped

1 cup red onion, chopped

½ cup red wine vinegar

1 cup extra-virgin olive oil

1 tsp rock or sea salt

Cracked black pepper

PARRILLA GRILLED BEEF SHORT RIB

Each rack of beef short rib should come with 4–5 ribs. Allow one rib per serve.

At El Matador we steam the short ribs for 3 hours before we grill them. Another pre-cooking option is to slow roast the short ribs in a deep oven pan. Cover the base of the pan with 3cm of red wine or water flavoured with a bay leaf, peppercorns and 2–3 whole cloves of garlic. Cover tightly with tin foil and cook at 140°C for about 3 hours. Check the meat after about 1½ hours, adding more liquid if the ribs are drying out, and re-cover tightly. You should have a nice moist and steamy environment under the tin foil. Once the ribs are cooked, let them rest for 30 minutes – this helps relax the meat and keeps the juices in the muscle.

To roast, season the meat lightly with salt and pepper and cook on a wood-fired barbecue or parrilla (pronounced pa-ree-a) for about 10 minutes until golden brown. You can either grill the whole rack or cut it into individual ribs with a sharp knife between the bones before you grill. If grilling the whole rack, let it sit a little after grilling before separating the ribs. Serve topped with Chimichurri (see page 104).

TIP | The ribs can be pre-cooked the day before and finished off on the barbecue just before serving.

Serves 4–5
Dairy free, gluten free

INGREDIENTS

1 rack of beef short rib, roughly 2.5kg

Red wine or water

1 bay leaf

Small handful of peppercorns

2–3 garlic cloves

Salt and pepper

CHURROS WITH CHOCOLATE SAUCE

CHURROS | Combine the caster sugar and cinnamon in a shallow bowl and set aside. In a medium saucepan, bring the water and butter to the boil. Add the flour, then reduce to low heat and stir with a wooden spoon for 4–5 minutes. Don't let the mixture stick to the pot. Take the pan off the heat, pour the mixture into a bowl, and let it cool for 5–10 minutes. Add the eggs one-by-one and mix until everything is combined.

Prepare for frying by filling a piping bag with the churro mix. A piping bag with a star nozzle (1.5–2cm wide) is a must for great churros. The bigger the nozzle, the thicker the churros.

Heat the oil in a deep-fryer or saucepan to 180–190°C and start piping the mixture straight into the hot oil. Pipe 3–4 strips at a time, snipping off each strip using scissors or a knife. Don't overfill the fryer. Cook the churros for 3–4 minutes or until golden brown. Remove with a slatted spoon or wooden chopsticks and drain the excess oil. Toss in the cinnamon-sugar mixture. Serve warm with El Matador Chocolate Sauce.

EL MATADOR CHOCOLATE SAUCE | Heat the cream in a saucepan and bring to the boil (don't let the pan overflow). Remove from the heat and add the chocolate and rum, whisking until smooth. Pour into a bowl and serve with the churros.

TIP | If you don't have a deep-fryer you can use a saucepan with about 4cm of vegetable oil. Cooking with hot oil can be dangerous so never leave it unattended. If you don't have a cooking thermometer you can test if the oil is hot enough by dropping in a cube of bread – it should brown in 30–40 seconds. If the oil gets too hot, just remove the pan from the heat for a while.

Makes 80 small churros
Vegetarian

INGREDIENTS

Churros

480ml water

170g butter

270g flour

7 eggs, size 6

1½ tsp ground cinnamon

½ cup caster sugar

Vegetable oil for frying

El Matador chocolate sauce

300ml liquid cream

350g good-quality 70% dark chocolate

1 shot of rum

149

CONSTRUCTED 1897

Designed by architect
Guido Schwartz

The building was designed and
built for a well-known brewer and
entrepreneur, Thomas George
Macarthy. In the years since it has
housed a diverse range of occupants,
including a boot seller, hatter,
watchmaker and stationer. Between
1924 and 1945, various fishmongers
occupied the space, beginning with the
Greek Pippos Brothers. Around 1995
it was used as a temporary premises
for Midnight Espresso while that café
underwent earthquake strengthening.
Today it's a jewellery shop, Lazulé
(since 2005), with upstairs offices
for Fidel's Café and Havana Bar.

181

CONSTRUCTED 1916

Designed by architect
James Bennie

The Art Deco building was
constructed for the Queen's
Theatre Co. It was seen as one of
Wellington's finest movie theatres
at a time when cinema was the main
form of mass entertainment in New
Zealand. It opened as the Queen's
Picture Theatre and operated under
a variety of names before closing
in 1955. After that, the building was
adapted for various uses, including
a billiard saloon, grocer's and other
retail stores. By 1980 the ground
floor of the building had found
sustained use as a café. Today it
is home to Loretta restaurant.

192

CONSTRUCTED 1917

Designed by architect
Claude Plumer-Jones

The building was designed for
the National Bank and remained
a bank for almost 80 years. In
1996 the first floor was converted
to the well-known Logan Brown
restaurant, still in occupation, with
an apartment on the second floor.

This beautiful, classically designed
building still retains its original
internal features, including the main
banking chamber, ornate ceiling
and dome.

201

CONSTRUCTED 1901
Designed by architects
James McKay and Rob Roy McGregor

The building was originally constructed as a dental practice for George Alford Downes and William Stacey Downes. It was designed with a waiting room, workroom, chloroform room and scullery on the ground floor, and a surgery, two further waiting rooms, a workroom and bathroom on the first floor.

The building was converted to a house, or possibly a boarding house, in 1935, and was re-named the Desmond House Apartments in the 1940s. It was altered by A. P. Littlejohn in 1958 into a restaurant that became Orsini's, one of Wellington's most significant dining establishments.

The opening of the restaurant coincided with the relaxation of the liquor laws. David Burton, a local restaurant owner and food writer, wrote of Orsini's: "Until 1961, when the government relented on its stupidly puritanical restaurant liquor ban, Orsini's had been forced to operate as a sort of speakeasy where patrons brought grog concealed beneath their coats. The front door was kept locked against police raids.

Having smuggled in full bottles of spirits as well as wine, patrons would proceed to drink themselves comatose in the downstairs dining area, perhaps appropriately, since it originally served as the Downes brothers' chloroform room."

Orsini's was the second Wellington restaurant to be granted a liquor licence. It flourished in the 1960s and became well known as a fine-dining restaurant of the type reserved for special occasions. Orsini's closed in 1990 and the building has since been occupied by a succession of restaurants.

There have been some recent alterations to the Cuba Street façade, including the 1997 conversion of the Diocletian or arched-headed window into French doors, and the addition of doors in the centre of the façade.

227 CUBA STREET
GRILL MEATS BEER

You could describe Grill Meats Beer as the casual and colourful baby brother to Logan Brown. Just a little further up Cuba, it's open to the street and will entice you in with its wide selection of beers and grilled food.

For those of us who like the occasional beer but have no idea how to move beyond the supermarket line-up of lager or ale, then Grill Meats Beer is the perfect place to go. With eight beers on tap and an ever-changing array of bottled choices from Porter to Pilsner, there's no excuse not to find something new and perfect to go with your food. Grill Meats Beer feels like a safe place to dip one's toes into the ever-growing world of craft beer. With names like Juicehead, Bird Dog, Magic Bean Stout and Witzig, who wouldn't be keen to give these beers a go? You can either read about them on the restaurant's chalk board, or the staff will guide you through the range of beers on offer.

The name Grill Meats Beer conjures up images of manly helpings of meat and beer; but fear not, there's plenty on the menu to please those of us less inclined to digest hefty portions of protein. For all that, the one thing Grill Meats Beer does particularly well is the burger, a forte that makes them a logical contributor to Burger Wellington, an annual event that challenges cafés and restaurants throughout Wellington to match their most creative burgers to a unique range of Garage Project beers. Pete Gillespie of Garage Project describes the challenge as "a competition based on the simple premise that the only way you could possibly make a burger better is to add a can of beer". It's hard to argue with that!

Left: Simon Coard and Marcus Bird

GARAGE PROJECT

What strikes you when talking to Pete Gillespie about Garage Project is his passion for pushing the boundaries of beer-making.

You could say it started back in 2011 when Pete, his brother Ian and mate Jos made 24 beers in 24 weeks with a glorified homebrew kit. Their ambitious project to release a new beer every Tuesday at 5pm created a fan base for what would come to be called Garage Project.

Seven years on and Garage Project has grown. With more than 50 employees, it's pretty busy. Their staff include a range of talented specialists who make the beer, sell it, market it and design the labelling. Pete is quick to acknowledge that their success is down to the calibre of the staff Garage Project attracts – like gravity!

The connection between beer and food is important. Garage Project likes to match beer with food, and believe their beer is an integral part of the Wellington culinary scene. The relationship is best showcased at the Wellington on a Plate beer and burger challenge, Burger Wellington, where every year three new beers are created to match burgers, providing a range that can go with most foods. Pete loves the collision of low and high culture that the challenge creates, and the winners get a beer brewed just for them.

Independent brewing is not a new concept in New Zealand, but it's pretty new in Wellington. It's growing at a fantastic pace, with many new breweries now sharing the scene with Garage Project. An increasing number are opening brew bars, where you can watch the beer being made as well as drink it. Some would say Wellington is the craft beer capital of New Zealand – cheers to that!

Left: Ali Rage Ali   Right: Pete Gillespie

POPCORN FISH WITH BURNT ORANGE AÏOLI

BURNT ORANGE AÏOLI | Zest the orange, then cut in half and coat with sugar on the cut side. On a grill or stovetop, heat a cast-iron skillet to medium-high. Cook the orange cut-side down until very dark, then remove from the heat and cool. Juice the orange and set aside. For a quicker recipe you can use fresh orange juice instead of caramelising the orange.

Place the mayonnaise in a bowl and stir through the garlic and orange zest. While stirring, add the orange juice gradually to avoid making the aïoli too runny – it should be thick and creamy. Season with salt to taste.

POPCORN FISH | Pat the fish dry with a paper towel and cut into bite-size pieces, approximately 1cm square. There should be about 8 pieces of fish per serving. Combine the fish flour ingredients in a bowl, and toss the fish pieces in the flour to coat.

To make the batter, place the tempura flour in a large bowl, gradually adding the soda water and ice and whisking constantly until smooth. Heat a large frying pan with about 3cm of oil to a medium heat. Dip the fish pieces into the batter and coat well, shaking off any excess batter. Fry a few pieces of the fish at a time for 2–3 minutes on each side or until golden brown. Drain on a wire rack. Serve with the burnt orange aïoli.

Serves 4

INGREDIENTS

Burnt orange aïoli

1 orange

2–3 tsp sugar

1 garlic clove, crushed

250g whole-egg mayonnaise

Salt

Popcorn fish

300g hoki, blue cod, blue warehou or any firm white fish

Vegetable oil for frying

Fish flour

½ cup tempura flour (or ¼ cup plain flour, ¼ cornflour and a pinch of salt)

1 tsp Szechuan peppercorns, ground

½ tsp salt

Batter

1 cup tempura flour

½ cup soda water to mix

1 small handful of ice

PORTER BRAISED BEEF BRISKET

Preheat the oven to 150°C. Season both sides of the brisket with salt and pepper. Heat a large frying pan with a tablespoon of cooking oil and brown the onion, carrot and celery. Place the vegetables in the bottom of a deep oven tray. Brown the brisket in the same frying pan until sealed. Place the browned brisket in the oven tray, on top of the vegetables.

Combine the remaining ingredients and pour over the meat. Top up with beef stock or water until the bottom of the pan is well covered. Heat the oven tray on the stove top, bringing the liquid to the boil.

Cover the brisket with baking paper or tin foil, then cover the oven tray with a lid to seal it. Braise in the oven until tender, about 2–3 hours or until a skewer goes through with no resistance. Turn the meat over halfway through cooking. When done, let it cool in the oven dish overnight if possible, or let it rest for 30 minutes if serving straight away. The meat will continue to cook while it's cooling down.

To serve, remove the brisket and strain the braising liquid. Reduce the braising liquid in a small saucepan until deep and rich, while skimming off the fat. Add extra water if necessary. Cut the beef into individual portions about 1cm thick and drizzle over the reduced braising liquid. If the meat has cooled overnight, warm it in the braising liquid before serving.

Serve with pickles, grilled bread and a dollop of mustard.

Serves 4–6

INGREDIENTS

1.5–2kg beef brisket

1 tbsp cooking oil

2 medium onions, roughly diced

2 large carrots, roughly diced

2–3 stalks celery, roughly diced

1 handful fresh thyme

2 garlic cloves, crushed

1 bayleaf

2 tsp sea salt flakes

½ tsp black peppercorns, freshly ground

250ml Emersons London Porter or any dark beer

Beef stock or water

To serve

Pickles

Grilled bread

Mustard

SALMON TERIYAKI WITH SOBA NOODLES

Serves 4

To make the marinade, combine all the ingredients in a small saucepan. Bring to the boil, reduce heat and simmer 4 minutes. Set aside and let cool completely. Transfer the marinade to a large bowl and put in the salmon. Cover and refrigerate 1–2 hours or overnight.

To make the broth, bring all the ingredients to a boil to dissolve. Cool and strain. The broth can be made ahead of time and heated just before serving.

Cut the marinated salmon into equal portions. Heat a drizzle of oil in a frying pan and cook the salmon for about 5 minutes on each side (depending on its thickness), turning only once. Cook the skinless side first. Turn the heat down to medium-low halfway through cooking. Once cooked, allow the fish to rest in the pan for 10 minutes before serving. You can prepare the noodles, broth and garnish while the salmon is cooking.

Finely grate the daikon and carrot into a bowl. Rinse under cold running water for a few minutes, drain and set aside. Thinly slice the roasted red pepper and set aside.

Cook the soba noodles in 2 litres of rapidly boiling water for 3–5 minutes, stirring all the time to prevent the noodles sticking together. Drain and rinse under cold running water.

Bring 2 litres of water to a boil and cook the shiitake mushrooms for 5 minutes. Cool, drain and slice if using whole mushrooms. Chop the bok choy into small pieces and add with the noodles and cooked mushrooms to the broth. Heat through.

Fill individual bowls with a serving of noodles. Spoon over the broth but don't completely cover the noodles. Place the cooked salmon on top, then garnish with sliced red pepper, toasted sesame seeds and the grated daikon and carrot.

INGREDIENTS

450g fresh salmon

270g soba noodles

½ bunch bok choy

20g dried shiitake mushrooms

Teriyaki marinade

½ cup soy sauce

¼ cup brown sugar

1½ tsp fresh ginger, minced

1 garlic clove, minced

1 tbsp honey

1 tsp sesame oil

3 tbsp mirin

Soba noodle broth

1.25 litres chicken stock

300ml soy sauce

150ml fish sauce

150ml mirin

1½ tbsp oyster sauce

3 garlic cloves, chopped

50g fresh ginger, chopped

1 tsp caster sugar

1 tsp white pepper, ground

Garnish

1 small daikon radish and ½ carrot

1 small red pepper, roasted and skinned

Black and white sesame seeds, toasted

FIDEL'S

Fidel's Café is much more than a Cuba Street institution; it's parent to successful children Havana Bar and Restaurant, and Havana Brothers Bakehouse. It's also home to the unofficial Mayor of Cuba Street, Roger Young, and his business partner Potti Wagstaff.

The story of Fidel's is that of a young Tauranga man, Roger Young, who in the 1990s travelled up and down New Zealand looking for places to sell his watermelons. He found an opportunity at the Southern Cross Tavern, the then pretty shady but popular student and public bar just off Cuba Street.

One night while walking home after raffling watermelons at the Southern Cross, Roger noticed an old building near the top of the street. Something about the two-storey wooden building sparked his interest, and a few years later, when looking for premises for his latest venture – a pizza joint called Little Gringo's – he saw the 'for lease' sign on that same building and it felt like a strange kind of destiny. He quickly signed the lease. He's still there more than 20 years later!

Roger had always been drawn to the shabby, eclectic appeal of Cuba Street as it was in the 1990s, reminding him of Notting Hill and Camden Town, which he'd experienced on his London OE.

After four years of making pizzas, Roger sold Little Gringo's to the Southern Cross. When the landlord wouldn't let him out of the lease of the premises, he decided to set up a café. Inspired by what friends Geoff Marsland and Tim Rose were doing with Midnight Espresso, Roger went on to set up Fidel's in 1996.

Roger met Potti one night sheltering from a lightning storm on Abel Smith Street. The tequila was brought out and the friendship was cemented. At the time Potti was working as an architect and helped Roger set up Fidel's. Their working relationship was so successful that Roger invited Potti to become a financial partner.

When you walk into Fidel's you immediately notice an interior that talks to Cuba and the Cuban revolution. There's a multitude of portraits of Fidel and his fellow revolutionaries, the Cuban flag is boldly on display, along with many photographs of Cubans going about their business.

Right: Potti Wagstaff and Roger Young

Fidel's Café has grown since 1996, extending into the old Supercuts hair salon next door as well as the car park, which is used for outdoor seating. The kitchen has also grown, and much of the baking is done off-site in their Arthur Street bakehouse. Today, about 40 staff work for Fidel's.

It's pretty obvious that Fidel's is making the most of being on a street called Cuba. But it's more than that. There's something about the café's aesthetic that is at home on the street. It has a friendly openness, a relaxed ethos, and the food, much of it organic, vegetarian or vegan, feels good for you too. Even if the menu is not typically Cuban (although the coffee is!), you'd be forgiven for thinking you're in a little corner of Cuba – the only thing missing is the free-flowing rum and the live salsa band.

Roger and Potti have been feeding the people of Cuba Street for over 21 years and today their influence continues with the Havana Bar and Restaurant just around the corner on Wigan Street, and the Havana Brothers Bakehouse on Arthur Street.

TIM TAM CAKE

A Fidel's classic and a stunning special-occasion cake. Find an excuse, invite some people around, and celebrate!

Preheat the oven to 160°C on a low fan. Lightly mix the oil, sugar, eggs and vanilla until smooth. Pour in the boiling water and cocoa powder and mix again until smooth. Mix in the ground almonds, baking soda and a pinch of salt.

Pour into a greased 23–26cm cake tin and bake for about 1½ hours or until an inserted skewer comes out clean.

Let the cake cool before cutting it in half horizontally. Spread half of the dulce de leche on the bottom layer and cover with the top. Spread the remaining dulce de leche or your favourite chocolate icing over the top layer. We also garnish our cake with freeze-dried raspberries for a dramatic look.

TIP | If you halve the recipe you can make one medium cake or 16 cupcakes. If making cupcakes, bake for 20–25 minutes.

Gluten free, vegetarian

INGREDIENTS

260g canola oil

400g sugar

6 eggs

2 tsp vanilla essence

100g cocoa powder

250g boiling water

300g ground almonds

2 tsp gluten-free baking soda

Pinch of salt

1 can of dulce de leche, either store bought or made by boiling condensed milk in the tin for about 60 minutes

To garnish

Freeze-dried raspberries

HAVANA BAR AND RESTAURANT

Havana Bar and Restaurant must be the Cuba district's coolest offspring. Housed in two historic cottages on Wigan Street, just off Cuba Street, it was once the hangout of Havana Coffee Works, originally the coffee roasting side of Midnight Espresso café.

When Havana Coffee Works decided to concentrate on their roasting business rather than the bar, they asked their mates Roger and Potti at Fidel's if they wanted to take it on. They did, and Havana Bar was born. A few years later, when Havana Coffee Works moved the roastery to Tory Street, Havana Bar opened a restaurant in the second cottage. Executive chef Mark Rawlins has worked at the restaurant since it opened in 2010. Some would say he's wedded to the business – he even got married there! He shares the kitchen with Kirran Buckland, a talented Kiwi chef just back from working in top restaurants in London, Edinburgh and Dublin. While it's easy to enjoy Havana Bar and Restaurant simply for its delicious tapas and drinks, its roots still remain deeply entrenched in cool vibes and live music, a legacy that continues today with three new gigs every week.

Left: Kirran Buckland and Holly Gulliver   Right: Mark Rawlins

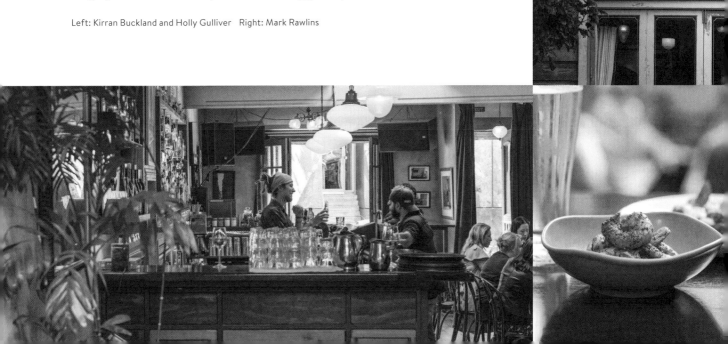

CRISPY OX TONGUE

Serves 6–8 as a tapas dish

This is a great party dish for anyone who likes to experiment and impress friends and family. Some elements will need to be made a few days in advance but will last a long time in the cupboard or fridge.

BUCKWHEAT | Mix the buckwheat, yoghurt, water and salt in a bowl and cover loosely with a tea towel. Leave in a warmish place for 4–5 days. Strain off the liquid then place the buckwheat on a baking tray lined with paper. Dry in the oven at 60°C for 3–4 hours until fully dry. In a medium pan heat 6–8cms of oil until close to smoking point. Watch carefully as it's dangerous to leave the pan for too long. With a dry slotted spoon, puff up the buckwheat in the oil for 5 seconds then scoop out and place on paper towels to dry. Season with salt.

BRAISED OX TONGUE | Bring 5 litres of water and the tongue to a simmer and skim. Add the vegetables and herbs and simmer for 3–4 hours until the tongue is very tender. Put aside until the tongue is cool enough to handle. Peel the tongue with a sharp knife by guiding it under the skin to remove the layer of rough skin. Trim off the fatty parts on the underside. Roll tightly in cling film to form a log shape. Cool in the fridge overnight.

OYSTER MAYONNAISE | Blend the egg yolks, water, oysters and vinegar. While blending, slowly add the oil until the mixture thickens. Season to taste.

SEMI-DRIED TOMATOES | Halve the tomatoes and place on an oven tray. Top with oil, salt and seeds. Bake at 60°C for 2–3 hours until semi-dried.

TO SERVE | Cut the tongue into 1cm slices. Pan-fry in a little oil until slightly crispy then place onto paper towels. Lightly sprinkle with salt flakes. Put the tongue on a serving plate, then pipe on the oyster mayonnaise and place the semi-dried tomatoes on top. Scatter sliced, pickled white anchovies around the plate. Sprinkle with the puffed buckwheat and garnish with your favourite herbs – we use wild fennel fronds, micro coriander and watercress. Finish with a drizzle of olive oil.

INGREDIENTS

Fermented puffed buckwheat
200g buckwheat
1 tsp cultured yoghurt
1 litre water
1½ tsp salt
Oil for puffing buckwheat

Braised ox tongue
1 fresh ox tongue
2 carrots, medium diced
2 onions, medium diced
5 garlic cloves
2 tbsp fresh thyme
½ bunch parsley
1 bay leaf
½ celery, roughly diced
1 leek

Oyster mayonnaise
3 egg yolks
50ml water
2 oysters and their juice
75ml black vinegar
300ml olive oil

Semi-dried tomatoes
200g cherry tomatoes
1 tbsp celery seeds
Olive oil, to drizzle
Sea salt flakes

Pickled white anchovies and herbs, to garnish

HAVANA BROTHERS BAKEHOUSE

It was because of rum that another member of the Fidel's family of cafés came into being. A commercial unit bought beside the Wellington bypass was primarily intended for storing rum imported from Cuba and providing a place for the boys to play poker. But a need for more kitchen space for Fidel's and Havana Bar saw the unit being put to work as a commercial kitchen, juicery and café, called the Havana Brothers Bakehouse.

Fidel's has always served fresh juice, but after discovering the superior taste and goodness of cold-pressed juice, Roger invested in a cold-press juicer. Finding it couldn't make anywhere near the quantities he needed, he installed the cold press that squeezes the Havana Brothers juices, and the food revolution just got bigger. A passion for fresh and organic produce was a good fit for this new venture: you could say that Roger's humble beginnings selling watermelons has come full circle!

Then there's the café at Havana Brothers Bakehouse. It's one of the best spots off Upper Cuba street for a coffee and healthy bite. It has both inside and outside seating, and is surprisingly sheltered and pleasant considering its position near the motorway bypass. It's become something of a coffee-house hub for many in the community, and is a favourite destination every Friday for the women of Never Stop Dancing, a dance workout class held in Cuba Street's Thistle Hall. These classes, run by Virginia Keast, are enthusiastically supported by many, and the energy these women bring to the Bakehouse after their class is infectious!

Right: Never Stop Dancing dancers Catherine Pearless, Christina Daniela, Roanne Potts and Maria Pippos

BANANA SPELT LOAF

This loaf strikes the perfect balance between a sweet treat and a hearty bread, the wholemeal spelt flour bringing a wholesome nutty bite. The loaf is great fresh, but even better toasted in a hot pan or sandwich press with a little butter.

Preheat the oven to 170°C. Mash the bananas in a large mixing bowl. Add the butter, caster sugar, brown sugar and egg, and mix until combined. In a separate bowl, mix together the cinnamon, baking soda, salt, plain flour and wholemeal spelt flour.

Fold the dry mix into the wet mix and lightly bring together. Try not to over-mix, as this will produce a tougher loaf. Pour into a buttered or oil-sprayed loaf tin (24 x 11cm) and bake for 60–75 minutes, checking with a skewer for a clean crumb. Cool in the tin for 20 minutes, then transfer the loaf onto a wire rack to cool further before slicing.

Serve with your favourite butter and berry compote.

Makes 1 loaf
Vegetarian

INGREDIENTS

540g very ripe bananas, peeled weight

115g melted butter

160g caster sugar

160g brown sugar

1 large egg

1½ tsp cinnamon, freshly ground

1½ tsp baking soda

Pinch of sea salt

185g plain flour, sieved

185g wholemeal spelt flour

240 CUBA STREET
LAUNDRY

Laundry is the story of three best mates with a passion for house parties and live music. As skilled tradesmen, they were able to transform an old dry cleaners on upper Cuba Street into a seriously cool place for 'eats and beats'.

Laundry is perfectly at home on Cuba Street. Grungy yet welcoming, the bar's decor is eclectic, rocking a 1960s chic meets junk-shop quirk. The caravan kitchen out the back miraculously serves up delicious soul food right out of New Orleans.

Two years after opening, Greigh was hired as manager to help Laundry make the most of what the three friends had established. Big on experience, this tall, bearded Canadian was able to articulate the ethos of Laundry and help put that ethos into place. Today Laundry is many things – café, bar, restaurant, nightclub, community hangout and modern-day speakeasy. The demographic is broad, but its core of regulars are artists, musos, hipsters and hospos, popping in for a late night drink.

A particularly well-known regular is Geoff Stahl, or DJ TV DiSKO as he's known at Radio Active, Wellington's alternative radio station. Not only is he DJ for the vinyl-only show, 'Music Without Subtitles' and an incredible user of alliteration (check out his page on Radio Active's website), but he's the customer who invented Laundry's legendary vegan pulled-pork burger. As part of the annual Garage Project Burger Wellington challenge, Laundry asked its regulars to contribute a recipe, and Geoff's (see page 142) proved so popular it's been on the menu ever since.

Left: Greigh McGrenera and Geoff Stahl

What really makes Laundry special is its contribution to the Wellington music scene. Craig Smith, partner at Laundry and passionate supporter of local music, works hard to provide a place for musicians and DJs to strut their stuff. The venue might be small, but it's big on atmosphere. There's an ever-changing and eclectic line-up of music, both local and international.

With their combination of food and music, Laundry has created an experience that evolves throughout the day and well into the night. Several times a week when diners have finished eating, the tables are magically cleared away, the light show warms up, and the party really begins. With the music pumping and the dance floor heaving with happy people, it's hard not to have a great time at this Cuba Street hangout.

At Laundry the puns flow almost as freely as the music and beer, with the likes of 'Money Laundering' as the name of a fundraiser gig and 'Dirty Laundry' for regular DJ spots. This playful language speaks volumes about the staff. Working here requires energy and plenty of personality, and being an extrovert certainly helps. When asked what they get out of what they do, the answer was simple: "We love it when people leave with an experience in their pocket". Hooray to that!

Left: Lucy Minter, Chris Allman and Greigh McGrenera
Right: Patrick Mackey – The Housing Project, Radio Active

GUMBO

Laundry's gumbo is the perfect dish for a large group of people.

Finely chop the garlic. Cut the capsicums, celery, okra, lotus root and potatoes into 1–2cm chunks and put aside. Finely dice the onion and cut the chorizo into 1cm-thick half-moons. Fry the onions with a pinch of salt and a drizzle of oil in a large pot (a big soup pot works well). When the onions begin to soften, add the chorizo and fry for 5 minutes or until its fats are released. Add the chicken and fry for 5 minutes. Throw in the chopped garlic and vegetables and fry a further 5 minutes.

Stir in the chipotle paste, cumin and Cajun spice. Pour in the vegetable stock to cover and add the sugar and vinegar. Bring to the boil and cook until the potatoes are tender. Season with salt and pepper to taste.

We serve our gumbo in bowls garnished with chopped kale and grilled prawns. It's also delicious with rice, couscous or fresh bread on the side.

TIP | You can find lotus root and okra at most Asian supermarkets.

Serves 15–20
Dairy free

INGREDIENTS

4 garlic cloves

2 red capsicums

1 green capsicum

2 celery sticks

1 bag frozen okra

1 bag frozen lotus root

1kg red potatoes (skins on)

3 onions

500g chorizo (5–6 sausages)

1 tbsp canola oil

1kg chicken thigh, diced

2 tbsp chipotle paste

5 tbsp cumin

6 tbsp Cajun seasoning

1–2 litres vegetable stock

3 tbsp soft brown sugar

¼ cup cider vinegar

Salt and pepper

To serve (optional)

Handful of chopped kale

3 grilled prawns (per serving)

TV DiSKO'S VEGAN PULLED PORK BURGER

When customers were asked to contribute to the Burger Wellington challenge with recipes, Geoff Stahl, a vegetarian customer, submitted this one and it's still on the menu. Some vegans think it tastes too much like pork!

Finely dice the onions and garlic. Heat a drizzle of oil in a large, heavy pot and cook the onion and garlic until soft. Add the cumin, smoked paprika and chipotle powder and sauté for 2 minutes. Add the tomato paste and ketchup and sauté another 2 minutes.

Add the cider vinegar and liquid smoke and stir to combine. Add the dates, Worcestershire sauce and tomatoes to the pot and let simmer for 30 minutes on a medium heat, stirring occasionally, until reduced. Whizz the sauce with a stick blender until smooth and season with salt and pepper to taste.

To rehydrate the bean curd, either blanche it in a pot of boiling water with salt and a drizzle of oil or follow the instructions given on the packet. Drain the bean curd once it has softened. Cool in iced water and drain again. Stir the bean curd into the blended barbecue sauce and set aside to cool. Keep in the refrigerator until ready to use – it's best left to marinade for a day before cooking. Just before serving, stir-fry the bean curd until it's cooked through.

At Laundry we serve our Vegan Pulled Pork Burger in buns with pickles, coleslaw and mustard.

Serves 10
Vegan

INGREDIENTS

1 red onion

½ white onion

4 garlic cloves

1 tbsp canola oil

1 tbsp cumin powder

1 tbsp smoked paprika

½ tbsp chipotle powder

2 tbsp tomato paste

2 tbsp ketchup

1½ tbsp cider vinegar

1–3 squirts liquid manuka smoke

¼ cup dried dates

2 tbsp Worcestershire sauce

400g can chopped tomatoes

Salt flakes

Cracked black pepper

250g dried bean curd sticks
(we recommend Double Dragons)

Iced water

To serve

Bread buns

Pickles

Coleslaw

Mustard

EKIM BURGERS

People love dining al fresco at Ekim Burgers, the established food truck near the top of Cuba Street. With Wellington's weather not always warm and sunny, it's impressive that such outdoor dining works all year round. This seems to be a reflection of the optimism of the average Wellingtonian.

Ekim was set up by Mike Duffy (Ekim is Mike spelt backwards). Starting out with a small food truck in Lyall Bay, Mike moved the business to upper Cuba Street, primarily to escape the cold southerly winds. He eventually sold the business to friend Mike Marsland, who saw in Ekim an opportunity different from any of the eateries he'd previously been involved with.

So what is it about Ekim that works? It's the fresh, open-air environment, the improvised décor, and the delicious burgers. This definitely isn't a posh place to dine, but the burgers are made from scratch with quality ingredients. In short, the food tastes good and is popular with families, retired people, tradies and hipsters alike. There's something very egalitarian about burgers!

The menu is surprisingly long, and includes burgers with names like McFilla, Honest Rob and Trevor. Usually three people work each shift; four at weekends. Sometimes you can see them dancing in the food truck as the orders flow in. So how busy is this buzzy spot on the corner of Abel Smith and Cuba? At the weekends this little food truck will make around 500 burgers a day.

Right: Jack Holland

HONEST ROB'S BEEF BURGER

BEEF BURGER | Combine the mince, garlic, salt, pepper, mustard, panko breadcrumbs, oregano and chilli powder in a large bowl and mix well. Divide the mixture into 6 parts and form into balls, then gently flatten to make patties. Keep covered in the fridge until it's time to barbecue. Cook at a medium heat on a pre-heated barbecue until done to your liking. While the burgers are cooking, grill the bacon rashers.

To build the burgers, spread Ekim's tomato sauce on the base of the bun and top with lettuce, onion and aïoli. Add the pattie, bacon, cheese, gherkins and salsa. Spread mustard on the top bun and place on top of the fillings.

EKIM'S TOMATO SAUCE | In a large pot, sauté the onions, garlic, chilli, coriander, cumin and bay leaves for 3–4 minutes. Add the canned tomatoes, roasted red pepper, vinegar, sugar, salt and pepper. Bring to the boil while stirring so the tomatoes don't stick to the bottom of the pot. Lower the heat and let simmer for 30 minutes, stirring frequently. Put the pot aside to cool slightly. The sauce can be puréed with a stick blender or left chunky. Season with salt and pepper to taste.

This recipe makes a couple of generous jars of sauce and will keep in the fridge for a week. It tastes great in any burger or on your homemade chips.

EKIM'S BLUE CHEESE AÏOLI | Combine salt, pepper and egg yolks in a blender or in a bowl if using a kitchen whizz. Blend for 2 minutes until thick and pale. Slowly add the oil – dribble a teaspoon at a time until the mixture thickens. Be careful to add the oil slowly as the aïoli can easily split. Once the mixture thickens, add the lemon juice or vinegar a tablespoon at a time. Once combined, remove from the blender and gently whisk through the mustard and garlic. Season to taste. Add as much of your favourite blue cheese as you can handle. Crumble into the aïoli and gently whisk through. Add a little at a time and taste. This recipe makes a small cup of aïoli that will keep for about 5 days in the fridge.

Makes 6 burgers

INGREDIENTS

Beef burger

500g premium beef mince

2 garlic cloves, chopped

1 tsp salt

1 tsp ground pepper

1 tsp whole grain mustard

½ cup panko breadcrumbs

1 tsp oregano

½ tsp chilli powder

6 burger buns

Burger toppings

Bacon rashers

Ekim's tomato sauce

Lettuce leaves

1 red onion, finely sliced

Ekim's blue cheese aïoli

Cheese, sliced

Gherkins

Jalapeño salsa

American mustard

TIP | For a simpler aïoli use ready-made whole-egg mayonnaise and simply add blue cheese.

INGREDIENTS

Ekim's tomato sauce

1 small onion, diced

4 garlic cloves, crushed

½ tsp chilli flakes

½ tbsp coriander seeds, blitzed

½ tbsp cumin powder

1 small bay leaf

800g canned tomatoes

125g roasted red pepper, sliced

2 tbsp balsamic vinegar

½ tbsp sugar

½ tsp salt

½ tsp peppercorns, ground

Ekim's blue cheese aïoli

½ tsp salt

½ tsp peppercorns, ground

3 egg yolks

1 cup olive oil or soya oil

3 tbsp lemon juice or white wine vinegar

1 tsp Dijon mustard

3 cloves garlic, crushed

Blue cheese

39 ABEL SMITH STREET
SOUTHERN CROSS

Just off the intersection of Abel Smith and Cuba streets, the Southern Cross Garden Bar Restaurant, or the Cross as it's more informally known, is definitely at home in the Cuba Street district. It's a community-friendly restaurant, bar, garden, social club, and much more. It has been a family-run business since 1989.

Those of us who were students in the 1980s will affectionately remember the Cross as the local, and may remember our shock when things started to change. As Wellington's commercial landscape altered, reinventing the tavern became essential. For a start, it needed a facelift – the public bar was pretty shady and the garden bar was definitely on the grunge spectrum.

In a bid to find a new market, Gary and Liz Clarke decided to create an experience that rivalled staying at home on the couch – a comfortable place with food, drinks and entertainment, and where women felt welcome. A greater emphasis was placed on food, family and community activities. There were a few experiments with getting food into the bar, starting with Little Gringo's and then, in 1992, Zebos. Eventually they opened their own restaurant in what used to be the public bar at the front. It took a while for locals to embrace it, but today it's extremely popular, especially at weekends.

The site was further developed by John Mills Architect in 2005 and 2006, and today includes a large garden bar and a variety of interesting spaces designed to fill a range of needs for different community activities, from life drawing to live music, knitting to salsa dancing. Gary and Liz's vision of creating a place where people could be a guest in their own home is very much a reality.

Right: Barry McGrath

CUBANFUSION'S SUNDAY SALSA

The Sunday Salsa Sessions at the Southern Cross bring a genuine touch of Cuba to the district, with Cuban dancer and musician Rafael Ferrer Noel and wife Rosina van der Aa's free monthly salsa class and dance party.

Eleven years ago, the Cross ran a series of dine and dance events featuring four different dance styles. CubanFusion – Rafael and Rosina's dance school – was asked to participate. Their salsa section proved so popular that it become a stand-alone monthly event and has been going strong ever since. Rafael and Rosina love that the free classes help people step outside their comfort zone and give dancing a go. They've enjoyed watching people change over the years as their dancing has improved. It's now the longest-running free salsa event in New Zealand, with around 200 people joining them on the dance floor each month. The dance school, like the Cross, is a family business. Son Sjaak has come to these events since he was a baby, and now aged nine, he's already a dancer and performer and sometimes helps out at classes.

How did a Cuban guy end up in Wellington? Rafael is from Havana and met Rosina while she was there for a film festival. Having spent eight years in Latin America, Rosina is a fluent Spanish speaker and experienced salsa dancer. Their mutual love of film, dance and music meant they spent a lot of time together. After leaving Cuba, Rosina ended up working in Mexico, and they were able to continue their relationship. When Rafael proposed marriage, they moved to New Zealand. Rafael joined Rosina in Wellington on 10 October 2005 – Cuban Independence Day. Every year at the Cross they celebrate the anniversary of Cuba's independence and Rafael's arrival in New Zealand. His strong presence in the Wellington dance and music scene has been fantastic for spreading Cuban culture in Wellington.

Left: Sjaak Ferrer van der Aa and Mauricio Alzugaray Vela, Rafael Ferrer Noel and Rosina van der Aa   Right: Greg Pollard, Lizzy Bee and Grant Major

HERB-CRUSTED LAMB WITH SALSA VERDE POTATOES AND LAMB SHANK RAGOÛT

Allow plenty of time to make this recipe. It can be prepared a day ahead and heated just before serving. The lamb loin can be grilled or roasted instead of using the sous-vide method.

SALSA VERDE | In a food processor, combine all the ingredients except the oil. Slowly drizzle in the oil while mixing until it reaches a nice pesto-like consistency. Season with salt, pepper and more vinegar if needed.

LAMB SHANK RAGOÛT | Roughly chop the parsley stalks, garlic, onion and carrot and sauté in a large pot. When the vegetables have a little colour to them, add the lamb shanks. Brown the shanks on all sides and then de-glaze the pot with the red wine. When the wine has come to the boil and started to reduce slightly, add the thyme and stock. Bring back to the boil and then turn down to a very gentle simmer. Cover with a baking paper cartouche and then tin foil. Let simmer on the stovetop or in a 150°C oven for 3 hours until the meat falls from the bone.

Remove the pot from the stovetop or oven and leave to cool. When the shanks are cool enough to handle, remove the meat from the bones and shred roughly by hand. Reduce the cooking liquor until thick and glossy. Return the shredded meat to the thickened jus and reserve until ready to serve.

SOUS-VIDE LAMB LOIN | Trim any silver-skin or fat from the loin and vacuum pack. Set the sous-vide water bath to 56°C. When it's at temperature insert the packaged lamb and cook until the internal temperature is about 55°C. Leave at this temperature for a minimum of 1 hour and a maximum of 4 hours. When the lamb has cooked,

Serves 4
Gluten free

INGREDIENTS

Salsa verde

2 garlic cloves, peeled

2 cups Italian parsley leaves

1 cup fresh basil

1 cup fresh mint

¼ cup capers

¼ cup gherkins

6 anchovy fillets

1 tbsp Dijon mustard

3 tbsp red wine vinegar

8 tbsp extra-virgin olive oil

Lamb shank ragout

2 lamb hind shanks

2 litres good quality beef or lamb stock

2 cups red wine

Stalks from parsley used in salsa verde

3 garlic cloves

2 onions

2 carrots

1 sprig thyme

200g edamame beans

Sous-vide lamb loin

4 x 180g lamb backstrap/loin pieces

4 tbsp Dijon mustard

Iced water

remove the bag and, still sealed, place into an ice bath until completely cooled. When the lamb is cool, open the bag and drain any cooking juices. Place on a paper towel until ready to serve.

HERB CRUST | Blitz the herbs in a food processor until finely chopped. Add the breadcrumbs and combine. Add the melted butter and seasonings and blend until a green paste/crumb forms. Spread onto an oven tray lined with baking paper and cover with another sheet of baking paper. Roll with a rolling pin until 3mm thick. Place in the freezer for a couple of hours until it hardens. When set, cut into rectangles to match the size of the lamb loins.

VEGETABLES | Boil the potatoes until tender, then drain. Stir the salsa verde through the potatoes and set aside. Peel the baby carrots and simmer for 6 minutes in salted boiling water, then take them out and put aside. Plunge the spinach in the left-over carrot water then pat dry in a clean tea towel. Season the blanched spinach with salt and pepper.

ASSEMBLY | Brush each piece of lamb with mustard and place a strip of herb crumb on top. Heat the salsa verde potatoes in a frying pan until they start to crisp at the edges. Warm the lamb shank ragoût in a small saucepan and fold through the edamame beans. In a separate frying pan, warm the lamb loins on the meat side only – don't over-heat as the lamb is already fully cooked. When the lamb is heated through, remove from the pan and carve into two pieces. Glaze the baby carrots in the pan used for the lamb.

Serve the dish with the potatoes on the bottom and the lamb loin on top. Place the shank and edamame ragoût in a heap next to the potatoes. Finish with the spinach and baby carrots.

Herb crust

1 cup gluten-free breadcrumbs, or regular if preferred

3 tbsp melted butter

½ bunch basil

½ bunch mint

½ bunch parsley

Salt and pepper

Vegetables

1 bunch baby carrots

500g washed and picked spinach leaves

1kg baby gourmet agria potatoes

SALTED CARAMEL VEGAN CHEESECAKE

In preparation for the filling, soak 2½ cups of cashews in warm water for at least one hour, or for even better results, overnight.

BASE | In a food processor, whizz the dates, melted coconut oil, cacao nibs and macadamia nuts until chunky and sticking together. Press the mixture into the bottom of a push-out tray and pop into the freezer to set while you prepare the filling.

CASHEW CHEESECAKE FILLING | Mix the soaked cashew nuts, melted coconut oil, vanilla, lemon juice and syrup in a good blender for about 5 minutes. Stop and scrape down the sides a few times during the blending. Spread a 2cm layer of cheesecake filling on top of the base. Return the tray to the freezer.

SALTED CARAMEL | Mix the cashew nuts, dates and salt flakes in a blender for about 5 minutes while drizzling in the syrup. Stop and scrape down the sides a few times. As you near the end of blending, slowly pour in the water to get a smooth caramel consistency. Add more salt and syrup to taste. Fill a piping bag with the caramel and pipe onto the set cheesecake filling. Garnish with chopped macadamias. Return to the freezer to set. Thaw for 10–20 minutes before serving.

TIP | This recipe works well for mini cheesecakes made in lined muffin tins or mini flan rings. Each base should be 1–1.5cm thick, topped with a heaped tablespoon of the cashew cheesecake filling. Finish with the piped topping and garnish with chopped macadamia nuts.

Makes 1 large cake or 15 mini cakes
Gluten free, raw, vegan

INGREDIENTS

Base

2 cups Medjool dates (340g box)

5 tbsp coconut oil, melted

½ cup cacao nibs (optional)

2 cups macadamia nuts

Cashew cheesecake filling

2½ cups cashew nuts, soaked

½ cup melted coconut oil

1 tbsp vanilla essence

2 tbsp lemon juice

¼ cup agave syrup or maple syrup

Salted caramel

1½ cups raw cashew nuts

2 cups dates, chopped

1 tsp sea salt flakes

150ml maple syrup

½ cup water

Garnish

Macadamia nuts, chopped

A PARTY WITHOUT **cake** IS JUST A MEETING

GLUTEN FREE
Lemon + Blueberry
Friand
$4.50 each

Lemon + Raspberry
$3.20 / $5.50

White Choc
Macadamia
$3.20 / $5.50

Caramello
$3.20 / $5.5

Caramel Toffee
Pop

Caramel Choc
brownie sandwich
$7.00

Lemon Slice
$6.00

Lemon + Raspberry
Slice
$6.00

VEGAN
Peanut Butter
choc brownie
$5.50

VEGAN
Peanut Butter
brownie sandwich
$7.00

268 CUBA STREET
SWEET BAKERY & CAKERY

Originally a lawyer working in managed funds, Grace Kreft has always gravitated towards baking. If there was a staff morning tea or special occasion, Grace was there with her baking, a passion she's had since she was a 10-year-old growing up in Wellington.

A trip to Britain on an OE gave Grace the opportunity to park being a lawyer and give baking as a career a go. With no professional experience, she was fortunate to get a job with a London cupcake bakery, Crumbs and Doilies. After a year she'd learned a lot about baking and running a business.

When Grace and husband Brad Kreft returned to New Zealand in 2013 they were keen to set up their own baking business. They started making cakes to order, and a year later set up the Karori Sweet Bakery & Cakery. Grace is the company director in charge of the sweet stuff and Brad is in charge of deliveries, logistics, and the artistry behind their cake toppers.

The next step was to find a retail space in central Wellington. Having visited the pop-up store promoting Whittaker's new K Bar, they saw the potential of taking over the lease – and Sweet Bakery & Cakery was born. The building is a heritage building moved to make way for the motorway bypass and has the unusual claim-to-fame of having one of the largest sash windows in New Zealand. Grace was attracted to its character details, including the remnants of its previous life as a butchery.

Grace still gets excited by the magic of baking and the chemistry of mixing ingredients to create something both delicious and beautiful.

Left: Helena van Echten Right: Demi Rose and Grace Kreft

LEMON AND RASPBERRY SLICE

Pre-heat the oven to 180°C fan bake. Line a large deep baking tray or tin (approximately 20 x 30cm) with baking paper.

Blend the shortbread ingredients in a food processor until combined and it forms a soft dough. Press the dough evenly into the lined baking tray or tin – it should make a layer of about 1.5cm. Set aside while you make the topping.

To make the lemon topping, whisk together the eggs and sugar in a bowl. Add the flour, then while whisking pour in the lemon juice and mix until smooth. Pour the topping over the base and scatter frozen raspberries evenly over the top.

Bake for approximately 35 minutes or until the lemon topping is just golden on the edges and set. Allow the slice to cool in the tray, then dust with icing sugar and garnish with freeze-dried raspberries (optional). Cut with a sharp, hot knife to serve. The slice will be easier to cut if chilled in the fridge overnight.

Makes 12 slices
Vegetarian

INGREDIENTS

Shortbread base

450g plain flour

150g caster sugar

350g softened butter

Lemon topping

4 eggs

260g caster sugar

60g plain flour

⅔ cup lemon juice

¼ cup frozen raspberries

Garnish

Icing sugar and freeze-dried raspberries (optional)

276 CUBA STREET
MARTHA'S PANTRY

Owner Mary McLeod originally wanted what is now Martha's Pantry to be an artist's studio that sold coffee.

The restored heritage building that houses Martha's Pantry was bought by Mary's great-aunt Martha and great-uncle John Moran in 1920, where they ran a drapery and lived upstairs. A woman known for her hospitality and excellent cooking, Martha kept her pantry under the stairs – next to where Martha's Pantry tearoom is now. Today the building is home to the next generation's businesses. The Moran's grandson runs the jewellery shop at the front of the building and Mary runs Martha's at the back.

Mary initially chose the space at the back because its light made it a perfect artist's studio. However, her artistic plans were dashed when she had to move to Hawera to help look after her brother's hotel. Daughters Anita and Ondine stepped in, and in 2007 opened Martha's. It was a felicitous fit: Ondine is a trained chef and Anita had worked at Deluxe Café.

Martha's is themed as a vintage tearoom and going there is like visiting your grandma for afternoon tea. The menu is classic Kiwi fare, with goodies such as scones, club sandwiches and lemon meringue pie. The teapots are covered in knitted cosies and the tea is served in fine china that would make any grandma proud. Customers have been known to gift fine china to Martha's, adding to the impressive collection of teacups. Martha's is the perfect place for a birthday tea, hen party or family get-together. It also has a number of loyal and loved regulars who make it a weekly highlight to treat themselves to a special afternoon tea. Today, Martha's is again run by Mary, who has resisted – for now – turning it into an artist's studio!

Right: Mary McLeod

NANA ADA'S CLUB SANDWICHES

Nana Ada always had these club sandwiches ready whenever she was expecting visitors for morning or afternoon tea.

CLUB SANDWICHES | Butter the bread slices (we prefer Molenberg bread) and spread some mayonnaise on the first layer. Add the lettuce and place another slice of bread on top, buttered side down. Butter the top of this piece, then add tomatoes and black pepper to taste. Add another slice of bread, once again buttered side down, and butter the top of this piece. Spread on the filling of your choice and top with the last piece of buttered bread. Remove the crusts and cut into three fingers for serving.

SAVOURY EGG FILLING | Mix together the hardboiled eggs and mayonnaise. Add curry powder to taste. Season with salt and white pepper.

CORNED BEEF FILLING | Spread store-bought or homemade cauliflower pickle (see recipe below) on a sandwich layer and top with sliced corned beef.

CAULIFLOWER PICKLE | Cut the cauliflower into very small pieces and place, together with the onions, in a large non-metal bowl. Sprinkle with the salt, cover and leave for 24 hours in a cool place. Next, drain the liquid and rinse with cold water. Blend the mustard powder, flour, turmeric and water, and put this in a large shallow pot. Add the sugar and vinegar to the pot and bring to the boil. Add the mustard seeds and rinsed vegetables and simmer slowly for at least 1½ hours, stirring regularly until the vegetables are soft and the mixture is thick. Transfer into sterilised jars and seal immediately. This recipe makes 3 or 4 500ml jars.

Makes 3 club sandwiches

INGREDIENTS

4 slices of light grain bread
Mayonnaise
Iceberg lettuce, finely cut
Tomatoes, sliced
Cracked pepper

Savoury egg filling

2 hardboiled eggs
Curry powder
Mayonnaise
Salt and white pepper

Corned beef filling

Cauliflower pickle
Corned beef, sliced

Cauliflower pickle

1 large cauliflower
1kg brown onions, sliced
2 tbsp salt
2 tbsp mustard powder
½ cup plain flour
40g turmeric
2 cups water
2 cups sugar
6 cups malt vinegar
½ cup yellow mustard seed

LEMON MERINGUE PIE

This is our most popular sweet treat and it's based on a Key lime pie. We had a regular customer who donated boxes of limes when in season, which prompted us to search for lime recipes – one can only drink so many gin and tonics! – and when limes were no longer abundant we used lemons instead.

Preheat the oven to 180°C. Melt the butter and mix in a bowl with the crushed vanilla wine biscuits. The consistency of the mixture should be dry. Grease a quiche or cake tin with baking spray or butter. Press the biscuit mix onto the sides and bottom of the tin, about 1.5cm thick. Bake for 12–15 minutes or until golden.

While the base is cooking, gently whisk together the condensed milk, egg yolks, lemon juice and zest. Pour the filling into the cooked base and bake another 12 minutes.

For the meringue top, whisk the egg whites until soft peaks form. Gradually add the caster sugar and continue whisking until the meringue mixture is firm and glossy. Pipe or pile onto the filling and bake for 10 minutes until the meringue is tinged golden. Cool before serving.

Serve on its own or with a dollop of whipped cream or yoghurt.

Serves 8–10
Vegetarian

INGREDIENTS

Base

100g butter

350g vanilla wine biscuits, crushed

Filling

560g condensed milk

4 egg yolks

3 lemons, zest and juice

Meringue

4 egg whites

½ cup caster sugar

CINNAMON OYSTERS

These soft and light little cakes are an old-fashioned favourite for afternoon tea.

Preheat the oven to 190°C. Grease patty pans and dust with flour, tapping off any excess. Beat together the eggs and sugar until the mixture has thickened and turned pale yellow. Warm the golden syrup in the microwave for 20 seconds and add to the egg mixture. Beat until well combined. Sift the flour, cornflour, ginger, cinnamon and baking soda over the mixture and fold through. Place tablespoons of the mixture into patty pans and bake for 10–12 minutes. Remove the cakes with a palette knife and cool on a wire rack.

Cut a slit into the side of each cake and fill with whipped cream. The cakes will taste best if they're filled with the cream a couple of hours before serving.

Makes 8 oysters
Vegetarian

INGREDIENTS

2 eggs

⅓ cup caster sugar

⅓ cup golden syrup

½ cup plain flour

1 tbsp cornflour

1 tbsp ground ginger

1 tsp ground cinnamon

½ tsp baking soda

Whipped cream

CUBADUPA STREET FESTIVAL

Cuba Street has long been home to an eclectic range of performers, beginning with the likes of the Perry Bros Circus in 1929 and continuing today with the regular flow of street performers who gather in Cuba Mall.

Once a year the Cuba district explodes into CupaDupa, a weekend of international and world-class local acts and performers. Lovingly curated, this free festival of music, street theatre, dance and art turns Cuba Street and its neighbourhood into a playground of delight. It's also when the eateries bring their food outside as part of the Moore Wilson's Street Food Festival, celebrating the street's many flavours.

The festival was established in 2015 by the Creative Capital Arts Trust as the vision of veteran festival-maker Drew James, building on the previous Cuba Street Carnival which ran from 1998 to 2009. At the heart of the festival is the desire to get everyone involved, blurring distinctions between performers and audiences – it's impossible not to get caught up in the music and dance in the street, or to join one of the many parades. Attracting over 100,000 people, it's an impressive feat of organisational flair and skill.

CupaDupa is a chance to experience all of Cuba Street at its most intense. Cuba Street is a unique asset, the result of a combination of many things: history, creative businesses and personalities, geography and architecture. Whatever makes this part of Wellington so special, one thing is certain: it's the perfect backdrop for this fantastic festival. Party on!

Left: White Face Crew performers Justin Haiu, Tama Jarman and Jarod Rawiri perform Pop Riders at CubaDupa Festival 2017. Pop Riders premiered at Pop 2016, Auckland Council

Right: Hilary Reid and the Wellington Batucada group and Greigh McGrenera

Photo credits: Amandala Photography, 2017 and Paul Taylor, 2017

Fresh Seasonal Produce

MOORE WILSON'S

Moore Wilson's is so much more than a place to get your bulk goods or fix of freshly squeezed orange juice. The wholesaler also offers an array of fresh, locally sourced produce and artisan products – it is truly impossible to shop there without buying more than you need! But what's most inspiring is the support Moore Wilson's gives to small, local producers, mentoring them and stocking their hand-crafted food and ingredients.

What has Moore Wilson's got to do with Cuba Street? This fourth-generation family business has been supplying many of Wellington's grocers, dairies and restaurants since 1918. They're also a passionate supporter of CubaDupa, sponsoring the Moore Wilson's Street Food Festival. The Festival is a way for eateries in the Cuba Street district to bring their food outside and be part of Wellington's biggest street party. Julie Moore, great-granddaughter of company founder Frederick Moore, sees their support of the festival as a chance to give something back to the community that has shopped with them for 100 years.

Moore Wilson's is a great place to buy local food, be it Havana Brothers' cold-pressed juices, Half Baked's vegan treats, or House of Dumplings' frozen dumplings. Oh, and in case you're stuck for where to get some of the more unusual ingredients listed in this recipe book, they have pretty much everything – from liquid manuka smoke to karengo seaweed.

Right: Graeme, Julie and Nick Moore

203

CONSTRUCTED 1904

Designed by architect
James O'Dea

The building was originally built for
Dr Patrick Mackin. Four years later
it was expanded by The Salvation
Army into the People's Palace
Hotel – the Army's traditional name
for its cheap, liquor-free hotels.
From 1916, The Salvation Army
leased the building as their national
headquarters before purchasing
the property in 1928, owning the
building until 1986. In the years
following, it became a number of
different hotels. Today it is part of
the larger CQ Hotel complex, with
the ground floor occupied by the
Cuba Street Bistro.

241

CONSTRUCTED 1908

Designed by architect
William Charles Chatfield

For many years the ground floor
was occupied by drapers, until the
mid-1930s to the 1970s, when it was
a grocery store – first Russell & Co.,
then Lewis's Store. The building
was purchased by the Wellington
Presbyterian Social Service
Association in the mid-1980s and
operated as an op-shop. In the
following years the space has been
used as offices for Havana Bar (2011)
and Swonderful retail store (2012),
before becoming Suite Gallery.

276

CONSTRUCTED 1907

Designed by architect
Charles Johnson

This commercial building was one
of many constructed in upper Cuba
Street following the commission of
the electric tramway in 1904. They
were intended to take advantage
of the increased traffic that the
tramways would bring. The building
has housed a number of businesses,
including an upholsterer, a fruiterer,
a ladies' and gents' outfitter, the
Regent Book Club, and Fashion Wise
Children's Wear. Today, the building
is occupied by the Jewel Centre and
Martha's Pantry vintage tearoom.

293

CONSTRUCTED 1907

Designed by architects
Francis Penty and Edward Blake

Thistle Hall was initially designed as a pair of shops and warehouse for William Campbell, owner of the Oriental Tea Mart. The cost of the building was £1,898.

Campbell sold the building in 1924 to the Protestant Hall Company, who converted the first floor warehouse into a social hall. The hall operated as the Empire Dance Hall and was also known as the Lodge Room, a meeting place for Wellington members of the Ancient Order of Foresters. From 1929, the building was threatened with demolition when there was a proposal to widen Arthur Street. Ownership of the building was transferred to the Equitable Building and Investment Company in 1943, and then to the Wellington City Council.

In 1951 the Council leased the hall to the Wellington Association of Scottish Societies (WASS) and the building was re-named Thistle Hall. Groups associated with the Scottish Societies included the Caledonian Society, Gaelic Club, Burns Club, Clan Cameron, and the Wellington Scottish Country Dance Club. The hall slowly fell into disrepair due in part to uncertainty about its future. Thistle Hall was sublet by WASS and from 1979–1981 became known as a punk music venue. It was also popular as an unlicensed venue where school-aged children could perform and attend gigs.

From 1987, Thistle Hall was the venue for community protest meetings against the demolition of properties in upper Cuba Street. Key activists included 'Save our City', a group that campaigned against the demolition of houses and small businesses in the area.

In 1989 the Council decided that although Arthur Street would be widened, Thistle Hall would remain. In 1989, Morehu Social Services took over its lease. Bookings included classes in Morehu Social Services cultural practices, jazzercise, women's self defence, tai chi, taekwon-do, Narcotics Anonymous meetings, work training seminars, after-school programmes for children living in the Arlington Street flats, and school-holiday programmes. The hall also continued as a live music venue.

In 1998 a group of local residents and business-owners formed a charitable trust to manage and run Thistle Hall. In 2002 the Trust obtained a Lottery Community Facilities grant of $11,000 to convert the retail units into a community-use art gallery and offices. Today, the earthquake strengthened and restored Thistle Hall is a thriving community building with a public gallery for hire and a hall used by various community groups.

THANKS

Wow! We made it to the top of Cuba Street. What a journey it's been for Fortyfive Design.

This book, as with any new baby, seemed like a good idea at the time but the reality, while rewarding, has been hard work! But like every parent, I am proud of what we've created. This book was a shameless excuse to be involved in an exciting, juicy and creatively unique project. As creative people we sometimes need to stoke our fires with work that challenges us and pushes us to try new things.

So why a book about Cuba Street restaurants and cafés? At the risk of sounding a little crazy, the idea landed in my brain and refused to budge. I suspect a long-time love affair with Cuba Street's cafés may have something to do with it. One thing is for certain: it was a great idea and we had a blast making it happen. We saw this book as a social documentary beautifully wrapped up with amazing recipes. The book is not a marketing exercise for the hospitality industry, and no one has paid us to make it. Its stories are the result of visiting the places we feature and talking with the people who work in them. It has taken us over a thousand hours of interviewing, writing, photographing, illustrating, typography, book design, recipe-testing, brainstorming, begging, food- and beer-tasting, and much more.

Right: Liane McGee

Many people have been instrumental in helping us along the way, but the following are the ones I'd most like to acknowledge:

I want to thank my two awesome graphic designers, Anna Vibrandt and Niki Chu for agreeing to embark on this crazy journey with me. They have worked with endless enthusiasm and brilliant design skill. Thank you too to Andrew McGee for your tireless support and help with some of the trickier photography. And finally, a mega thanks to Fiona Oliver for agreeing to edit the work of first-time authors. Your amazing editing skills have been the finishing touch to this book.

One of the things we most wanted to achieve was to make something beautiful, and we wanted to print it in Wellington. Our design studio has always preferred to use local printers, so we approached Blue Star Print Group and Spicers New Zealand for sponsorship. Their contribution both financially and professionally has been critical to helping us achieve the best possible result. We would particularly like to thank Paul Sutherland for being our go-to print guy and enthusiastic supporter throughout this project.

Undertaking a project to write, design and self-publish a book is not something the average person does. Once we realised that we had indeed bitten

off quite a bit, we were grateful for the advice various people gave us along the way. A super big thanks to our publishing mentor Sarah Bennett, her no-nonsense advice has been essential for keeping us on the right track.

We would also like to thank the following wonderful people for their help:

Lily Kao and Sarah Sun, Dong Zhang, Vicky Ha, Oliver Middleton, TK Ball and Yota Kojima, Lisa Tomlins and The Eggs, Leonardo and Lorenzo Bresolin and Lucas Tock, Karl and Sarah Tiefenbacher and Jo Healey, Julie Clark, Ben Bostock, Jamie Morgan and Ferdi Petagna, Scott and Maaike McNeil, Hamish, Zara and Shinee McIntyre, Geoff Marsland and Joe Stoddart, Marc Weir, Steve Logan and Shaun Clouston, Chris Walker, Sanjay Dayal, Mike Marsland and Andrew Wood-Calva, Roger Young and Potti Wagstaff, Mark Rawlins, Kirran Buckland and Holly Gulliver, Virginia Keast, Marcus Bird and Simon Coard, Pete Gillespie, George at the Cellar Door and Mattie Koenders, Greigh McGrenera, Geoff Stahl and The Housing Project crew, Jay and Jack at Ekim, Georgia Teague and Tim, Liz and Gary Clarke, Rosina van der Aa and Rafael Ferrer Noel, Grace Kreft, Mary McLeod, Drew James, Miett Fear and Charlotte Wooster, Julie Moore, Sarah Meikle, Rebecca Shannon and WREDA, Vanessa Tanner and WCC Heritage, Rex Nicholls, Fiona Gunter-Firth, Paul Taylor, Amandala Photography, Maree Bishop, Philip Kane, Coral Laughton and Brian Young, and anyone else we may have forgotten! Again, thanks.

Liane McGee, Fortyfive Design Studio